Daniel

Foundation for the Future

Marvin McKenzie

Published by Marvin McKenzie 2014

THE BOOK OF DANIEL, FOUNDATION FOR THE FUTURE

First edition

978-1-312-74680-0

Written by Marvin McKenzie.

Table of Contents

GIVING AWAY THE GOODS
Daniel 1:1-3

One of the "for-sureties" about God is that we do not understand
Him. Just about the time we think we have defined and
outlined and stuffed neatly in our preconceived box labeled
"deity" God does something that just does not make sense.
This book, written by its namesake, is a rare find in the pages of
mankind. We will find repeated over and again through this little
prophecy, evidence of such godly character that Daniel is set up
more than once in the Bible as an example of the great believers.

Ezekiel 14:14.
Though these three men, Noah, Daniel, and Job, were in it, they should deliver
but their own souls by their righteousness, saith the Lord God.

Ezekiel 28:3.
Behold, thou art wiser than Daniel; there is no secret that they can hide from
thee:

This is phenomenal indeed when we remember that Daniel had this
testimony in a strange land, having been stolen from:
- **His home**
- **His family and**

- His spiritual heritage.

Daniel is a Joseph type person.
- **He was unjustly taken**
- **In his youth**
- **To a foreign land**

- **Where instead of being bitter**
- **He surrendered his situation to the Lord and**
- **He prospered for God's glory**

But before we can properly understand the book of Daniel, we have to understand something of the history of Israel. Israel is a people that the Bible says God chose to set His love upon.
- **Not because they were the biggest**
- **Not because they were the most godly**
- **Not because they were the most wonderful people on earth**

God chose to love them because He chose to love them. God's love toward these people led to some amazing blessings.
- **God gave them a land flowing with milk and honey**
- **God enabled them to defeat the people of Canaan supernaturally**
- **God blessed them with great leadership under men such as Joseph, Moses, Joshua, David, and Solomon**

The trouble was, they got to a place where, as a nation, they thought they really were better than the other nations and that God could not help but love them and bless them. They could not fathom God ever judging or punishing them.

- **They were, after all, the apple of God's eye**
- **They were the only nation of people who worshipped the living and true God**
- **They were the children of Abraham and Isaac and Jacob**

They were so sure that God would bless them that they forgot that His people should also obey Him. And though God was gracious a very long time with them, there came a day when even their cup of iniquity was full.

God sent a particular prophet, Jeremiah to warn them that they were about to face the chastening hand of God and that they should submit to that hand. God, Jeremiah said, was about to send Nebuchadnezzar, the King of Babylon, to conquer them and to send them into captivity. Jeremiah's counsel, under the direction of God, was that Jerusalem should surrender to Nebuchadnezzar. If they did, God said, they would not suffer much and after a period of about 70 years, they would be allowed to return home from Babylon to Jerusalem.

Remember; Nebuchadnezzar was being sent as a chastening rod from God.

- **Israel had sinned against God**

- **She had been sinning against God for years.**

If she had humbled herself and repented and accepted her judgment we know exactly what God would have done.

1 Peter 5:5-6
.... God resisteth the proud, and giveth grace to the humble.
Humble yourselves therefore under the mighty hand of God, that he may exalt
you in due time: (KJV)

The record of God's word is that the Jews rejected Jeremiah's preaching. The Jews refused to surrender to Nebuchadnezzar, so God allowed him to soundly defeat the Jews, and they went into captivity anyway – only this time it was after much heartache and loss of life.

We know that Nebuchadnezzar actually attacked Jerusalem at least twice. It was during one of those raids that the story of Daniel begins. I want to show you from verses 2-3 of Daniel chapter 1 tonight, the cost of sin unrepented.

Verse two begins, "*And the Lord gave…*"
This just would not have been conceivable in the mind of the Jews that God would give anything worthwhile to Nebuchadnezzar – especially things that belonged to the Jews.

But God gave Nebuchadnezzar the most valued things of Israel. As a form of judgment against the Jews for not repenting of their sins God gave into the hand of Nebuchadnezzar.

JERUSALEM'S FIGUREHEAD
"...Jehoiakim king of Judah...."

This is a very big deal. He was the last king in David's family. God had made a promise to King David.

2 Sam 7:8-16

Now therefore so shalt thou say unto my servant David, Thus saith the LORD of hosts, I took thee from the sheepcote, from following the sheep, to be ruler over my people, over Israel:

And I was with thee whithersoever thou wentest, and have cut off all thine enemies out of thy sight, and have made thee a great name, like unto the name of the great men that are in the earth.

Moreover I will appoint a place for my people Israel, and will plant them, that they may dwell in a place of their own, and move no more; neither shall the children of wickedness afflict them any more, as beforetime,

And as since the time that I commanded judges to be over my people Israel, and have caused thee to rest from all thine enemies. Also the LORD telleth thee that he will make thee an house.

And when thy days be fulfilled, and thou shalt sleep with thy fathers, I will set up thy seed after thee, which shall proceed out of thy bowels, and I will establish his kingdom.

He shall build an house for my name, and I will stablish the throne of his kingdom for ever.
I will be his father, and he shall be my son. If he commit iniquity, I will chasten him with the rod of men, and with the stripes of the children of men:
But my mercy shall not depart away from him, as I took it from Saul, whom I put away before thee.
And thine house and thy kingdom shall be established for ever before thee: thy throne shall be established for ever. (KJV)

But now the sin of Jerusalem is so terrible that God, set this promise aside to deal with His people. God did not renege on His promise; He just put Israel in a "time-out." To this day there has been no leader in Israel after Jehoiakim related to King David.

The Bible tells us there won't be another until Jesus Himself sits on the throne. Using ungodly leadership is one of God's most common ways to chasten His people.

Proverbs 29:2
When the righteous are in authority, the people rejoice: but when the wicked beareth rule, the people mourn. (KJV)

We have seen a rash of wickedness in leadership in our world today haven't we? Everything from
- **Presidents who commit fornication in the White House**

9

- To business leaders who are unethical
- To parents who teach children to sin through their own example

We have a Chief of Police who is so corrupt that a man who was charged to protect the families of our area murdered his wife and then took his own life. What's more, we are losing our spiritual heritage here in the United States. It is becoming more and more common to play down the impact Christianity had on the foundation of our country.

- Our founding father's faith is being denied
- Our founding father's goals for our country are being ignored
- Our founding father's themselves are being lied about

And I am quite sure we can attribute it to the judgment of God upon our land. Americans have lived in such grace.

- We have wealth
- We have power
- We have prestige

world-wide. But we have forgotten God. And because of it I am afraid God has given our leaders over to the devil.

God gave into the hand of Nebuchadnezzar

THEIR ARTICLES OF FAITH

"...with part of the vessels of the house of God..."

Remember that the Jews did not worship God in the same fashion we do. Theirs was a system of rituals.

- **Each ritual was symbolic of a spiritual truth**
- **Each ritual was vital to their faith**

It will be worthwhile to remind you of the different items involved in their worship. The house of God was divided into three major areas.

A. The outer court

This area was walled and had a gate facing the east. Only the priests entered this courtyard area, and they did it on the behalf of the people of Israel.

As they entered the court, the first piece of furniture or "vessel" the priest would see was

1. The Brazen Altar

This is where the sacrifice was offered to God. No one draws near God without a sacrifice. Blood has to be shed to atone for our sins. This symbolizes for us the sacrifice of Jesus Christ on the cross.

After the animal was sacrificed and offered before the Lord the priest would approach

2. The Laver

This was a large vessel filled with water and having spigots to allow for running water to wash the priest's hands and feet. There was a large "catch bowl" around the bottom of it so the ground wasn't running with mud.

It reminds us that even though we are saved and forgiven our sins through the shed blood of Jesus Christ, we need to confess our sins daily before the Lord to remain clean and have good fellowship with Him.

Again, facing the east was the door to the Tabernacle's first room,
B. The holy place

Entering into this room to the right was
1. The golden lamp
The priests were responsible to make sure the light never went out in the Holy place. It is representative of Jesus Christ who is the Light of the world. It also reminds us of the Holy Spirit of God who enlightens the Word of God to our souls so we can understand God's way.

To the left was,
2. The table of showbread

The priests would place 12 fresh loaves of bread on the table every week. It represents Jesus Christ who said he was the "bread of life." It also reminds us that man cannot live by bread alone but by every word that proceeds out of the mouth of God. We desperately need to read and study and meditate on the Word of God.

Strait ahead and next to the holy veil was
3. The altar of incense
The priest would burn sweet smelling incense here, representing the prayers of the saints rising before God.

Only one man was ever allowed to go past the holy veil into
C. The Holy of Holies
And he was only allowed in their once a year. This was where the *Ark of the Covenant* was located. The ark was a box which contained three very important articles of Israel's spiritual heritage

1. The Ten Commandments written by the hand of Moses
2. Aaron's rod that budded
3. A bowl of manna

When Israel lost these, they lost what they considered to be the tools of their worship. From then on, all they ever did was "fake it." They made pretty things that looked similar but they never had the presence of God upon them again.

If we do not confess our sins and turn back to the Lord, He is likely to remove from us our ability to draw near to Him?

- **I know we can never lose our salvation**
- **I know that Jesus will never leave us nor forsake us**

But I also know that a Christian who lives with unconfessed sin realizes his relationship with God is broken.

- **He does not enjoy reading his Bible**
- **He comes to church but the messages seem as sounding brass**
- **He tries to pray but the prayers seem to bounce off the ceiling**

God gave into the hands of Nebuchadnezzar

JERUSALEM'S FAMILIES

Namely, their children.

Vs 3

And the king spake unto Ashpenaz the master of his eunuchs, that he should bring certain of the children of Israel, and of the king's seed, and of the princes; (KJV)

I don't like to endure hardships very much. But I will tell you what I don't like even more; I don't like seeing my kids endure hardships. Can you imagine the pain these Jews must have felt when Nebuchadnezzar began taking the very brightest and best of their

14

children away from them? We will see later that Daniel and his three friends did very well and lived to glorify God. But there would have been countless others who did not do so well.

Nebuchadnezzar's plan was to:
- **Take away their name**
- **Take away their heritage**
- **Take away their old beliefs and**
- **Take away their old lifestyle**

and teach them to live like him and serve for him.

You have to know there were a bunch of those kids that gave in to the pressures of
- **Wine**
- **Food and**
- **Worldliness**

Conclusion:

God gave into the hands of Nebuchadnezzar
- **Jerusalem's figurehead**
- **Jerusalem's vessels of faith**
- **Jerusalem's families**

All because the Jews refused to humble themselves and confess their sins before God and accept whatever chastisement God had for them.

- They thought they were all right
- They thought they could get by on their past grace
- They thought God would let them get away with their sin one more time

But not this time. Jeremiah had preached to them to surrender to Nebuchadnezzar. If they had obeyed the preacher, who knows what God might have done:
- Certainly He would have been gracious to them
- Certainly He would have protected them
- Certainly he would have blessed them even through their judgment.

And I know this, we would be far better off
- If we would confess to God our sins
- If we would humble ourselves and accept our chastisement and
- If we would leave ourselves in the hands of God's grace.

We might end up with:
- Better leaders
- A closer walk with God and
- A family that lives for the Lord with us

DANIEL: SELECTED FOR SERVICE

Daniel 1:1-4

Daniel was a Jewish boy from Jerusalem who was taken captive into Babylon around the year 605 BC. He is thought to have been of royal blood, which one of the reasons he was chosen to be taken into the king's palace in Babylon.

Nebuchanezzar was known to:
- **Take young men with leadership potential from the countries he occupied**
- **Train them in his philosophy and mentality**
- **Send them back to lead their own land on his behalf**

By doing that he was able to avoid some of the uprisings of the people.

But Daniel never did make it back to Jerusalem. He was taken captive, most likely in his late teens or early twenties and lived to be between 90 and 100 years old surviving Babylon's takeover on at least two occasions.[1] He wrote the book of Daniel around the year 535 B.C.

---

[1] WA Criswell, *Criswell Study Bible*, pg 976-977

While all who accept the Bible as the Word of God acknowledges that; no Old Testament book other than Genesis, is more contested than is the book of Daniel. The reason is simple. *The skeptics say it predicts the future governments of the world too accurately to have been written before the events took place.*

The book divides handily into two halves

1. The biography of Daniel
Chapters 1-6

2. The prophecies of Daniel
Chapters 7-12

Daniel is one of the most important books of prophecy found in the Bible. It is *"the skeleton of prophecy on which all other prophecy is placed"*[2] and is the key to understanding the rest of the prophetical books of the Bible.

I want to ask some indulgence of you. I want to make a leap that is, I know, difficult to swallow. I want to use King Nebuchadnezzar as a type of God.

[2] J Vernon McGee, *Thru the Bible*, Vol 3 pg 524-527

- **He is a king, a sovereign**
- **Our God is the sovereign**

Nebuchadnezzar knew that in order to have stability in his growing kingdom, he had to have a modicum of peace with the subjects of the various peoples and cultures he conquered. In an effort to do that, he would choose certain young men from each of these conquered lands and train them in his business. The work of these men would be significant. His success in choosing the right young men was key to the success of his kingdom. So these young men could be no slouches. They had to be top of the line.

The Bible says they were to be "*…certain of the children….*" (The word "children" is one that always means young men.) I want to use Nebuchadnezzar's standards for choosing these young men and use that to address the type of Christian most likely to be selected for service for Jesus Christ.

There are six standards listed out for Ashpenaz to search for in the children he brought to Babylon. I have divided those six into three groups.

Ashpenaz was to look at
THEIR STATURE

Vs 4
"Children in whom was no blemish, but well favoured...."

A. This idea of no blemish reminds me of the animal auction yards

When my mom and dad go to buy a new horse at auction.

1. The first thing they do is look at breeding.

They do that before they ever get to the auction. They trace down the bloodlines. When you have been doing it for any length of time, you recognize those horses whose blood is the best. You know the name of their granddaddy or grandmother; maybe even the name of their great granddaddy and mother. You might even know the name of some of the brothers and sisters and how well they have done in competition. But you can't buy the horse just on blood.

2. Then they check out the horse for general soundness.
- Is it healthy?
- Does it walk well?
- Are there any signs of physical deformity?

3. They check out their looks.
- Is it physically well proportioned?
- Does it stand well?
- Does it hold its head well?

- Is it pretty to look at?

Ordinarily stature has to do with one's physical build. But we know that the Lord "*looketh on the heart*"
1 Sam 16:7
But the LORD said unto Samuel, Look not on his countenance, or on the height of his stature; because I have refused him: for the LORD seeth not as man seeth; for man looketh on the outward appearance, but the LORD looketh on the heart. (KJV)

God isn't so interested in your physical appearance. But He is interested in your heart. Could your heart stand to the same scrutiny my parents give to a horse they are about to buy? None of us are perfect. I am glad that perfection is not the standard God uses when He selects those of us He will use in His service.

God has a right to expect us to be undefiled. God has a right to expect His children to be
- **Clean**
- **Pure**
- **Without blemishes of the world's wickedness and sin**

Then there is the phrase
B. Well favoured

In the context it has more to do with popular because of looks. But our God is concerned about something different than looks.

- **He is interested in our testimony**
- **He is interested in our reputation**

One of God's qualifications for the preacher is,
1 Timothy 3:7
Moreover he must have a good report of them which are without; lest he fall into reproach and the snare of the devil. (KJV)

If this is good quality for the preacher, it is a good one for us all!

THEIR SKILLS
Vs 4
.... skillful in all wisdom, and cunning in knowledge, and understanding science, ...

Nebuchadnezzar told him to find children who were

- **Skillful**
- **Cunning**

A. The word "*skillful*" means, among other things, "*expert.*"
What is wrong with the child of God getting to be an expert at something?

I know the Bible says, 1 Corinthians 1:26-28

.... not many wise men after the flesh, not many mighty, not many noble, are called:
But God hath chosen the foolish things of the world to confound the wise; and God hath chosen the weak things of the world to confound the things which are mighty;
And base things of the world, and things which are despised, hath God chosen, yea, and things which are not, to bring to nought things that are: (KJV)

But that doesn't mean we can't be

- **Educated**
- **Well read**
- **Students of good things**

We don't have to be hillbillies and backwoods people. There isn't anyone alive who couldn't improve their minds with a little'

- **Reading**
- **Study and some**
- **Formal education.**

I don't think the Bible is the only good thing to study. There are plenty of subjects that are worthwhile to learn. But certainly for the child of God knowing the Bible should be on the top of our list. May I ask you, what would be wrong with an average Christian being an "expert" in his Bible?

B. The word *"cunning"* means *"a thinker"*

23

1. God leads people to think.

Matthew 22:41-45

While the Pharisees were gathered together, Jesus asked them,
Saying, What think ye of Christ? whose son is he? They say unto him, The Son of David.
He saith unto them, How then doth David in spirit call him Lord, saying,
The LORD said unto my Lord, Sit thou on my right hand, till I make thine enemies thy footstool?
If David then call him Lord, how is he his son? (KJV)

2. God warns us to guard our thinking.

Proverbs 23:7

For as he thinketh in his heart, so is he: Eat and drink, saith he to thee; but his heart is not with thee. (KJV)

3. God tells us what to think about.

Philippians 4:8

Finally, brethren, whatsoever things are true, whatsoever things are honest, whatsoever things are just, whatsoever things are pure, whatsoever things are lovely, whatsoever things are of good report; if there be any virtue, and if there be any praise, think on these things. (KJV)

4. God tells us there is a reward for thinking.

Psalms 1:1-3

Blessed is the man that walketh not in the counsel of the ungodly, nor standeth in the way of sinners, nor sitteth in the seat of the scornful.

But his delight is in the law of the LORD; and in his law doth he meditate day and night.
And he shall be like a tree planted by the rivers of water, that bringeth forth his fruit in his season; his leaf also shall not wither; and whatsoever he doeth shall prosper. (KJV)

This is a skill any Christian can develop if they work at it a little bit. First, you have to have something to think about.

- **You get that by reading – say, the Bible**
- **You can simplify the process a little by writing down a verse you want to think about**
- **You might do a little research on the verse to stir up your thoughts a little**

And then, as you go about your day,

- **You think about the passage**
- **You pull it out once in a while and try to get every word down**
- **You think about the meaning of every word and how they relate to each of the other words**
- **You think about how the verse applies to you**

Usually people who think also have something worthwhile to say. Why not be an expert in the Bible and a thinker for the Lord?

THEIR SPIRIT
Vs 4
....., and such as had ability in them to stand in the king's palace, ...

A. The word "*ability*" means "*strength*" and the word "stand" has to do with how you present yourself.

I get the impression it means that presence a person has when they have confidence in themselves and what they are doing.

- **It has to do with your demeanor**
- **It has to do with how you are perceived**

These are young men who are going to stand before dignitaries and powerful people and represent the King. You don't want:

- **Someone who is unsure of themselves**
- **Someone who is timid**
- **Someone who is uncomfortable**

But neither do you want them to be arrogant and cocky. They can't overshadow the king they represent.

This is humility. A genuinely humble person has strength, but it is controlled. It is used by his sovereign.

Some time ago I was watching a horse show. I saw a young girl with her horse.

- **She was hugging on the horse's neck**
- **The horse was kissing her face**

You could tell the girl absolutely loved her horse and felt safe around it. But I know the horse has the physical strength to kill the little girl at any moment if it chooses. The horse had tremendous power, but it was broken – under the control of this far weaker little girl.

God is looking for some people who will be broken before Him. Who will put:

- **His goals**
- **His concerns**
- **His plans**
- **His desires**
- **His name**

above their own.

B. Look to see that they have the right birth.

Vs 3

....children of Israel, and of the king's seed, and of the princes; (KJV)

I am talking about those God selects for His service whether:

- **Full time service or a**
- **Volunteer ministry in His church or**
- **Just being used to bless those people they are around**

- **They ought to be pure and clean**
- **They ought to have a good report from the people who know them**
- **They should be experts in the word of God**
- **They need to be thinkers about the things of God**

- **They have to be broken and humble before the Lord**

But first of all, none of those will matter unless they are born into the right household. Jesus said it this way

John 3:7

.... Ye must be born again. (KJV)

ALIAS

Daniel 1:6-7

The Bible elevates Daniel to a status that very few in the Word of God hold. It gives us a good deal of the details of his life, and never once tells us about his sins. It is a sign of the truthfulness and infallibility of the Bible that it does not whitewash the sins of its heroes.

- **We know of Adam's sin**
- **We know of Noah's sin**
- **We know of Abraham's sins**
- **We know about the sins of Isaac and his sons Jacob and Esau**

- **We know about the sins of Moses, considered by many to be the greatest man in the Bible**
- **We know about the sins of Joshua**
- **We know about the sins of David**

- **We know about the sins of Peter, James and John**

God gives us heroes. But God does not sugarcoat their lives by any means.

- **Abraham, the friend of God lied about his wife**

- Moses, of whom the Bible says there was never a man like him who saw the face of God and lived, died in the wilderness because he became angry and presumed upon the Lord
- David, who the Bible says is a man after God's own heart, committed vile sins

But of Daniel,
- Whose prominence in the Bible is equal every bit equal to theirs, of whom the angel Gabriel said he is "a man greatly beloved"[3]
- Whose story is not quite as detailed and that of Moses and David, but still very detailed

There is not one word about
- A sin
- A failing
- A lack of faith

Daniel and his three friends were stolen, most likely as teenagers, from their homes in Jerusalem during the sieges of Nebuchadnezzar, King of Babylon. The four were:
- Of royal blood
- Well educated
- Very talented

young men; hand picked by Ashpenaz, the master of Nebuchadnezzar's eunuchs. His purpose was to train them in the

---

[3] Daniel 10:11

"learning and tongue of the Chaldeans" so they could become leaders in his kingdom.

Ashpenaz has the responsibility to get these boys indoctrinated in the Babylonian way of life and sell them on a life of loyal service to King Nebuchadnezzar. He has to somehow get the Israeli out of them and get the Chaldean into them. And the Bible says that the first thing he did **was to change their names.**

It has been several years ago now that I got a call.
- **A preacher I knew well when I was in Oklahoma**
- **A preacher I had had preach at the college**
- **A preacher who had taught classes**
- **A preacher was well thought of**

had been arrested. Over the course of the next several months it came to light that this preacher had been leading a double life. In public he was a well dressed:
- **High standards**
- **Strong preaching**
- **Moral man**

But he had a second life that was filled with:
- **Immorality**
- **Gambling**
- **Wickedness**

In order to pay for this double life, this preacher had been robbing banks. And that is how he was finally caught and the rest of it all came out.

You see,
- He did not go to the prostitute on the street and write her a check with his real name on it.
- He did not sit down at the blackjack table in the casino and introduce himself as "Pastor So and So

No in the daytime he was
- The pastor of this Baptist church
- The husband of this beautiful lady
- The father of those godly children

In the nighttime though, he went by an alias.

I led a guy to the Lord in Astoria who had been a pretty bad guy.
- He was a drug user
- He was abusive
- He was in a lot of trouble

I don't think I will ever forget. The day after we led him and his girlfriend to the Lord, she showed up at my office. Her boyfriend and her had gotten in a fight right after we led them both to Christ and he hit her. She told me that he was

- **Abusive**
- **A drug user**
- **In trouble with the law**

and asked me to counsel her. My first piece of counsel was never to let him in the house again. He was gone and good riddance. I told her I would only counsel her if she never missed a single church service – "miss one and we are done."

- **She listened to that and became very faithful to church**
- **She did not listen to me about the boyfriend and let him come back**

But she had a condition – he had to come to every single service with her. And he became very faithful and turned his life completely around. So much so that when we moved from Astoria, Anita and I trusted him enough that we rented our house to him and his wife. Anyway, he had what I thought was a funny practice that went back to his drug days.

- **His friends and family all called him Allen**
- **Everyone else called him Charles**

He had it that way so he knew which part of his life was trying to contact him. If a person called him on the phone and asked for *Allen*, he knew it was a friend. If the person asked for *Charles:*

- **It was a police officer**
- **It was a drug dealer**
- **It was a parole officer**

It was someone he did not want to speak to. Charles was his "alias."

Ashpenaz knew that if he ever hoped to get these young men to serve Nebuchadnezzar, he had to get them to forget their old lives. And they could never have done that with their real names. So he assigned each of them an alias.

You see, especially in those days, names were given with a purpose. There was a message, a lesson, even a heritage that a person carried with them through their name. The name Daniel, for instance, means *"God is my judge."* If Daniel had been allowed to keep that name, it would spell doom for Nebuchadnezzar's plan. Every time someone called for Daniel, he would remember that:

- **God was watching**
- **He would one day stand before God**
- **He would be held accountable to God**

So Daniel was assigned the alias, Belteshazzar. That means, *"Bel's prince"* or *"he whom Bel favors."* Bel was a heathen god of Babylon. Every time Daniel would be addressed by this alias,

- **He would be flattered – Ashpenaz thinks so highly of me**
- **He would be indoctrinated – our god is Bel**
- **He would be diverted-from worshiping the true God to this false one**

The name Hananiah means *"God has been gracious."* And that was something these four needed to be reminded of. You know, as tough as we might have things, we need to remember that God has been gracious to us and give Him thanks. If he were allowed to keep that name every time anyone called for him, he and his friends would remember to thank the God of Israel. They would never be genuinely loyal to Babylon. Ashpenaz assigned him an alias too. Shadrach means *"servant of Sin"* the moon god. His alias would make it possible for him to forget God's goodness and indulge himself in the worldliness he had been captured to serve in.

The name Mishael means, *"Who is equal to God?"* No way could Ashpenaz allow that name to be spoken. Can you imagine standing before Nebuchadnezzar, the king, who demands to be worshiped by his people as a god, and for him to call you *"Who Is Equal to God?"* If they were ever tempted to give in to the king's worldly ways, all that had to happen is one of the four called out Mishael's name and they would be reminded that Nebuchadnezzar is not equal to God. Ashpenaz assigned him the alias, Meshach. It means, *"The shadow of the prince."* Like Daniel's alias, this one was given to flattery.
- **I am somebody**
- **I am important**

I am the shadow of the very prince.

The name Azariah means, *"God has helped."* The Hebrews would call out Azariah and remember where

- **Their help**
- **Their strength**
- **Their power to overcome worldliness**

comes. Ashpenaz assigned him the alias, Abednego. This name is tied to the worship of the planet Venus and the goddess, Ishtar.

Go by their aliases and these four can travel all over the world in Babylonian days and do exactly as Nebuchadnezzar wishes them to do.

- **They can be as worldly**
- **They can be as wicked**
- **They can be as welcome in royal crowds as they please**

and no one will be the wiser about the God they were born to serve.

I want my name to be a name that leads people to Christ rather than excuses my life of worldliness.

I WANT A GODLY NAME

In other words, I want to have the type of testimony that when people think of me, they think of living for the Lord. Like the name, Enoch
Gen 5:24

And Enoch walked with God: and he was not; for God took him. (KJV)

I do not know for sure what people think of when they think of me. But I would like for them to think of me as someone who walks with God. There are a lot of things that are all right in this world. But I don't want anyone to associate any of that with me. I would like to live in such a way that the first thing that comes to mind when my name is mentioned is God. He walks with God.

What is it you think people think about when they think of you?
- **Is it your favorite hobby?**
- **Is it your favorite way to dress?**
- **Is it your favorite place to go?**
- **Is it what you do for a living?**

There isn't any reason why the thing people think about when they think of you and me is about the Lord.

A GOOD NAME
Proverbs 22:1
A good name is rather to be chosen than great riches, and loving favour rather than silver and gold. (KJV)

Closely associated but not the same as a godly name is a good name. I want to live my life in such a way that people think good things about me. Not for flattery's sake but:
- **Because I have been a friend**

37

- Because I have been faithful

- Because I have been kind
- Because I have been considerate

- Because I have been thoughtful
- Because of I been there for them

I was thinking the other day about the Lord Jesus Christ. No one was godlier than was Jesus.

Yet Jesus was also out among the people. His compassion and caring for people was obvious.
- He wept for them
- He provided for them
- He visited them
- He knew them
- He was patient with them
- He was truthful to them

A CONTINUING NAME
2 Timothy 1:5
When I call to remembrance the unfeigned faith that is in thee, which dwelt first in thy grandmother Lois, and thy mother Eunice; and I am persuaded that in thee also. (KJV)

Of 1,394 known descendants of Jonathan Edwards, of which

- 13 became college presidents
- 65 college professors
- 3 United States Senators
- 30 judges, 100 lawyers
- 60 physicians
- 75 army and navy officers
- 100 preachers and missionaries
- 60 authors of prominence
- one Vice-President of the United States
- 80 public officials in other capacities
- 295 college graduates, among whom were governors of states and ministers to foreign countries

Whatever walk with God I have and whatever testimony of goodness to men I have I want to pass it down.

- To my children and grandchildren
- To the members of my church and even
- To people in my community as I seek to win them to Christ, baptize them and teach them to live for the Lord

I want to have a godly name and a good name that is also a contagious name.

LIVING ABOVE THE CROWD

Daniel 1:1-8

Daniel was snatched from his home as a teenager. He surely was aware that those who had captured him had probably killed his own family as well as decimated

- **His homeland**
- **His friends**
- **His neighbors**

He finds himself:

- **In a strange land**
- **Under a strange culture**

Having no spiritual support other than that of some other young people in his same shoes. And yet we read of a young man of whom the Bible tells us:

- **No sin**
- **No fault**
- **No failure of any kind**

With virtually:

- **No support**
- **No hope of reward**

Facing terrible tribulation for his stands. Was able to keep his testimony before God so pure. The Bible says that Daniel *purposed in his heart that he would not defile himself with a portion of the king's meat, nor with the wine which he drank:*

It is interesting that Daniel took his stand on what some might call a little matter. Risking your life because you don't want to eat a particular food seems foolish.

I have two thoughts for you:
1. It is in the little things that the biggest compromises are made. It is the little sin that leads to the bigger ones. If we would never have given in to the smaller sin- we would likely never even be tempted with the largest ones. It would be tough for instance for the devil to come up to an innocent teenager and get them to rob a bank.

So he starts with smaller things.
- **He gets him to smoke a cigarette so he can be cool and fit in with the popular kids.**
- **Pretty soon those kids invite him to a party where he discovers they are smoking marijuana. He doesn't want to be laughed at so he takes a puff or two.**
- **After using the marijuana for a while, it is not that much of a step to smoke a harsher drug.**

The next thing he knows, he is hooked on something like Meth or Coke and his habit drives him to theft to pay for it. The easiest place to avoid huge sins is by refusing to indulge in the smallest sins.

2. Our temptations may not be the same, but it is just as important that we do not defile ourselves.[4]

I want to suggest to you that we have to purpose not to:

A. Defile our minds

Proverbs 23:7a

For as he thinks in his heart, so is he:

This has to do with what we subject our minds to.

- **The entertainment we take in**
- **The education we receive**

There are things we can "consume" into the mind that will never leave us.

God says,

Philippians 4:8

Finally, brethren, whatsoever things are true, whatsoever things are honest, whatsoever things are just, whatsoever things are pure, whatsoever things are

---

[4] These three sub points came from a sermon I found at http://www.rftpsermons.com/05272001am.html, accessed 2/4/06

lovely, whatsoever things are of good report; if there be any virtue, and if there be any praise, think on these things. (KJV)

We need to purpose not to

B. Defile our bodies

1 Corinthians 6:18-20

Flee fornication. Every sin that a man doeth is without the body; but he that committeth fornication sinneth against his own body.
What? know ye not that your body is the temple of the Holy Ghost which is in you, which ye have of God, and ye are not your own?
For ye are bought with a price: therefore glorify God in your body, and in your spirit, which are God's. (KJV)

This is why we ought not to:

- **Drink alcohol**
- **Smoke cigarettes**
- **Overeat**

The body belongs to God and ought not be controlled by anything other than the Lord. It is also why our young people ought to take the Bible seriously when it says *It is good for a man not to touch a woman…. but ….let every man have his own wife,*[5].

We need to purpose not to

---

[5] 1 Corinthians 7:1-2

C. Defile our souls

Mark 8:36

For what shall it profit a man, if he shall gain the whole world, and lose his own soul? (KJV)

That is not speaking about losing your salvation. That can't happen. But you can defile your soul so that it no longer is under the influence of the Holy Spirit but is controlled by the flesh and you do all sorts of wicked and abominable things. There is only one way to keep from being defiled. That is to purpose in your heart not to be defiled.

DANIEL'S PURPOSE PULSATED WITH CHARACTER[6]

Daniel purposed in his heart.

- **There was no one to make him do right**
- **There was every reason to give in to the circumstances**

But he purposed in his heart not to defile himself anyway.

---

[6] My main points for this message were found in a sermon I located at http://www.hobesoundbiblechurch.com/resources/outlines/050515.php, accessed 2/4/06

Someone said that character is what you are when no one is looking.

- **FEAR over-master FIDELITY.**
- **POLITICS corrupt our INTEGRITY.**
- **CUSTOMS become stronger than our CONVICTIONS.**
- **PLEASURES overpower our PRINCIPLES.**

Pleasures can be wrong when they become:

- **A PRIORITY for our living.**
- **A NECESSITY for our happiness.**

Daniel's character was demonstrated right from the beginning of the book, but it carried him through his entire life. Many people would like to do right. Only those who have character will get it done.

DANIEL'S PURPOSE WAS PUNGENT WITH COURAGE

Vs 5

The king appointed them a daily provision....

This was no little issue, this not eating the meat and wine. It was tantamount to disobeying his new king; the king who could have just as easily ordered his execution. It takes courage to purpose in your heart not to be defiled.

- **There will be those who mock and ridicule you**

- There will be opportunities in this world that you miss out on
- There will be friends who forsake you

When you purpose not to be defiled, when you purpose to do what is right, someone is going to see if they can't change your purpose.

1 Peter 4:4
Wherein they think it strange that ye run not with them to the same excess of riot, speaking evil of you: (KJV)

Just taking the stand to do right will take courage enough.

DANIEL'S PURPOSE WAS PROVEN IN CONFLICT
Vs 10-15

In other words, he was tested. Whenever we purpose not to be defiled, you can guarantee that the devil is going to do all he can to break our purpose.

1 Peter 4:12-14
Beloved, think it not strange concerning the fiery trial which is to try you, as though some strange thing happened unto you:
But rejoice, inasmuch as ye are partakers of Christ's sufferings; that, when his glory shall be revealed, ye may be glad also with exceeding joy.

If ye be reproached for the name of Christ, happy are ye; for the spirit of glory and of God resteth upon you: on their part he is evil spoken of, but on your part he is glorified. (KJV)

Everything of quality gets tested.
- **Cars get tested by smashing into thin walls**
- **Car batteries get tested by subjecting them to the elements of heat and cold**
- **Tires get tested by driving them nonstop from fiery sands of the Baja to the Tundra in Alaska**

There are companies that make their income just by testing products to see how they stand up.
- **Good Housekeeping**
- **Road and Track**
- **PC World**

All test products and report their findings to the consumers; you and me, who decide whether or not to purchase based on how well the products held up under testing.

A purpose that is not proven under testing is genuinely purposed. Daniels purpose was:
- **Pulsating with character**
- **Pungent with courage**
- **Proven by conflict**

DANIEL'S PURPOSE WAS POLISHED BY COURTESY
Vs 9

Jack Hyles wrote a series of books
- *Blue Denim and Lace*
- *Grace and Truth*
- *Strength and Beauty*

The proposition of each was that in every aspect of life there must be a measure of conviction that is softened with courtesy. I remember Dr. Hyles said that if he had to be either kind or stand for convictions he would rather stand for his convictions. It is better to stand for right and not be kind than to be kind and compromise the right.

But most of the time we do not have to make that choice. Most of the time we can keep our convictions and be kind at the same time. Someone said, "An incorruptible conscious does not necessarily imply a sour nature."

TEN TIMES BETTER

Daniel 1:1-20

Nebuchadnezzar was, for an unsaved man, a very wise leader. They say that at the age of 21, he had conquered the known world, and he is considered to be one of the world's greatest military geniuses.

One of these wise practices that Nebuchadnezzar had was to take several of the more promising young people from a country he had conquered and train them in his own palace. These young men would be fed from the king's table, be given all their needs for clothing and provisions from the king's own store, and be given a new name by the king.

After the young men saw all that Nebuchadnezzar had to offer and were convinced that a life of serving him would be a great life with many rewards and after they were properly educated, Nebuchadnezzar would assign them leadership positions- usually in their home country. By allowing natives to rule over countries he had conquered, Nebuchadnezzar was able to maintain a more peaceful rule over his large domain.

Daniel and his three friends were slated for that kind of training.

- **Nebuchadnezzar gave them new names.**
- **He also appointed them a daily provision of the king's meat and wine.**

All in an effort to convince the four to sell out to worldliness, I mean Nebuchadnezzar.

But Daniel had already sold out to another king. And because of his devotion to the KING OF KINGS AND LORD OF LORDS, Daniel purposed in his heart not to eat of the king's meat or drink of the king's wine. Melzar, the king's man to prepare them was justifiably worried. If Daniel and his friends weren't properly nourished, the king would notice and Melzar would be in for trouble. So Daniel proposed a test; He and his friends would eat the pulse (vegetables) and drink water for 10 days- if they were not healthy, they would be in Melzar's hand.

Not only were they healthy, verse 20 says that the king looked at Daniel and his friends and found them to be *ten times better* than all his magicians and astrologers that were in the land.

I don't know about you, but I long to be better. I am not too smart, but I am smart enough to know that I am not the best there is. I am not even the best that I can be. I want to be... I long to be *better*. I don't worry myself about being ten times better than others. I do want to be better, even ten times better than I am today

How about You? Wouldn't you like it to be said of you that you are ten times better than you were before? I want to suggest to you that there are ways to improve yourself;
- **In the sight of man, yes. But more importantly,**
- **In the sight of God.**

God is very much interested in our improving our standing before Him! In fact, I believe that God has included this story in Daniel so that you and I can learn from it how to be *ten times better.*

Consider first with me, that Daniel and his friends were ten times better,

BECAUSE OF THEIR TRAINING

We commend Daniel that he would not defile himself, but someone had to tell him that he would get defiled if he ate the King's meat and drank the king's wine. It should be obvious to all of us that *proper living is preceded by proper training.* One of the greatest needs in our world today is for people to teach what is right and wrong.

A. Begin at the home

With parents that set Biblical guidelines and make their children live within them. Parents are doing their children such a disservice to let them run wild. Kids need to learn right and wrong.

It should continue

B. Into their educational years

It does not seem reasonable to me to tell a child what is right and wrong and then turn them loose with a bunch of teachers and other children who will tell them not to believe your values.

It should continue further

C. Into the church you belong to

Where the Pastor should be willing to, and the church should give him the authority to, preach all that he believes should be preached. None of us will know how we can be defiled by wrong unless somebody tells us.

Worldliness will still defile you.

- **It is still wrong to eat the king's meat and drink the king's wine.**
- **It will defile you to compromise with this world and enjoy the pleasures of sin, even for a season.**

Daniel knew He would be defiled because he was properly trained on what is right and wrong. That training played a large part in making him ten times better.

BECAUSE OF THEIR FAITH

A. He believed his training
One of the reasons I believe in good training- one of the reasons I believe we should put our kids under godly teachers is because they will believe what they are taught.

Faith is believing something enough to live by it. All you need to do is look around at how the majority of people live and you can see they have faith in what their worldly teachers have taught them. On the other hand, look at Daniel and you see a young man who was taught right from wrong and had faith in it.

Romans 10:17
Faith cometh by hearing, and hearing by the Word of God.

We had better make sure we hear and our kids hear the Word of God.

Daniel also
B. Believed God.

Enough to put Him to the test.

I am afraid that a good many of us do not really have much faith in God.

- **Most of us are religious.**
- **Many of us are devoted to our church.**

But I am afraid that very few of us place a whole lot of faith in God.

The shame in that is that faith in God is so important.

1. It is through faith that we are saved

Ephesians 2:8

For by grace are ye saved through faith; and that not of yourselves: it is the gift of God: (KJV)

The Bible says *Abraham believed God and it was counted to him for righteousness.* (Romans 4:3)

Galatians 3:7 says

"they which are of faith,...are the children of Abraham"

The only hope for eternal life, the only hope you and I have for heaven is to believe God and come to Him His way; through Christ.

2. We are to live by faith
Galatians 3:11 says
"The just shall live by faith."

That means we believe God and act accordingly. It is wrong to say "I'm living by faith", if we are doing our own thing. Daniel and his friends were living by faith. They were practicing what they had been taught.

You will be living by faith when you too are practicing what you have been taught from the Bible.
- **It takes faith to go out and tell people about Jesus.**
    - **When we do it, we are living by faith!**
- **It takes faith to give your kids a Christian education.**
    - **When you do it, you are living by faith.**
- **It takes faith to give the tithe to the church.**
    - **When you do it, you are living by faith.**

3. Without faith it is impossible to please God
Hebrews 11:6

- **There is no salvation outside of faith in God**
- **There is also no lifestyle that pleases God but a life of faith.**

Faith is believing God enough to live His way.

BECAUSE OF THEIR OBEDIENCE

They did not just talk about right and wrong, they did what was right.

The Book of James tells us, *"Faith without works is dead."*

Praise the Lord. Daniel knew the truth of that.
- He had been taught that compromise and sin would defile him
- He had the faith to believe what he had been taught, and here we see
- He put his faith to work, and obeyed

A. He refused to compromise the principles of his faith

Whether it made the king angry or not, he would not compromise what was right.

Christians, we must learn that we do not well to compromise what is right with the world.
- We are NOT going to do any real good to put Christian words to the Devil's music.
- We aren't going to accomplish anything lasting to dress like the world and look like the unsaved, hoping we can win them that way.

Compromising with the world, just to keep them happy with us, will do no good.

B. Daniel also refused to give in to sin

That's the drinking of wine in Daniel's case. It is sin to drink an alcoholic drink, even in moderation, and even socially. When we commit sin, we become

- **Defiled**
- **Unclean**
- **Separated from God**

I believe in separation. I want to be separated from sin, but not from God. And we have that choice.

2 Corinthians 6:14-18

Be ye not unequally yoked together with unbelievers: for what fellowship hath righteousness with unrighteousness? and what communion hath light with darkness?

And what concord hath Christ with Belial? or what part hath he that believeth with an infidel?

And what agreement hath the temple of God with idols? for ye are the temple of the living God; as God hath said, I will dwell in them, and walk in them; and I will be their God, and they shall be my people.

Wherefore come out from among them, and be ye separate, saith the Lord, and touch not the unclean thing; and I will receive you,

And will be a Father unto you, and ye shall be my sons and daughters, saith the Lord Almighty. (KJV)

- If we have fellowship with sin, we do not have fellowship with God.
- If we have fellowship with God, we do not have fellowship with sin.

Which would you rather?

C. Daniel was rewarded for his obedience
vs 17

God gave them knowledge and skill in learning and wisdom so they were found to be ten times better than the magicians and astrologers.

GOD IS! And He is a rewarder of them that diligently seek Him.

How about you? Wouldn't you like God to reward you like this?

WISE MEN FAIL

Daniel 2:1-13

The book of Daniel has two major themes; the first has to do with character. As the Word of God describes to us how Daniel came to be stationed in Babylon, serving the kings of that nation, God's Word also gives us insights into the qualities that give a person exceptional character. Scattered throughout this book there will be clues to lead us toward godly character.

The second major theme, and by far the largest in the book, is the prophetic one. The book of Daniel is foundational to understanding everything else the Bible teaches concerning the future.

Chapter one is primarily focused on Daniel's rise to prominence in Babylon. It ends with a summary statement that incorporates Daniel's life all the way from Nebuchadnezzar through Cyrus. Chapter two skips back to the near beginning of Daniel's life in Babylon – to his first real crisis in serving the king.

I have a suspicion that regardless whether we are speaking about the politics of Babylon or the politics of Washington, working under leadership of that magnitude means "high stress" living. Certainly this was a high stress event. High Stress for the:

- **Magicians**
- **Astrologers**
- **Sorcerers**
- **Chaldeans**

High stress for Daniel and his friends too.

Dr. W.L. Smith, my prophecy teacher in college said concerning Nebuchanezzar's dream that troubled him,

- **"External prosperity in itself cannot secure peace of mind"**
- **"High rank is especially subject to restless anxiety"**

Proverbs 13:7
There is that maketh himself rich, yet hath nothing: there is that maketh himself poor, yet hath great riches. (KJV)

Say what you want to about me. I would rather have very little and be rich than be very rich and powerful and have nothing.

Our world places a premium on education. The educational system for all practical purposes defies education. Enough education, think those who defy education, will not only get a person a better job

- **It will cure social ills**
- **It will right moral wrongs**

- It will correct current errors
- It will bring man to a godlike status

Those in the educational field, even those who are involved in religious education, often view education as the answer to
- **Reducing poverty**
- **Converting criminals**
- **Eliminating world wars**

I want to tell you – wise men fail. Our faith had better not be in the wisdom of man – whether it is our own wisdom or the wisdom of another. There is only one who will not fail – that is Jesus Christ.

Nebuchadnezzar turned to his wise men in a troubling time and they failed him in three areas:

THEY FAILED IN FOCUS

The term wise men is used 8 times in our text but it is a general term for five fields of study. These men had focused on verse 2 gives us four of them. Each of the four overlaps to a degree into the others, but each of them has their own field of focus – specialty.

A. Magicians

The word means like an inscriber. These were people who practiced magic by drawing lines and circles. Pentagrams comes to my mind.

B. Astrologers

This was the practice of magic by the study and use of the stars. There is in the Bible a correlation between the stars and the supernatural and angelic beings. Satan and his devils most likely inhabit the stars. And one way to worship them is through the worship of the stars.

C. Sorcerers

These were those that whispered spells. They practiced magic through witchcraft and the use of familiar spirits.

D. Chaldeans

This word came to represent those who studied philosophy. All this reminds me of the educational system and their many "fields of study":

- **Liberal Arts**
- **The sciences**
- **Mathematics**
- **Physics**
- **Philosophy**
- **Economics**
- **Social Sciences**

These fields of study, unlike those in the book of Daniel, are not necessarily evil in and of themselves. But their focus will fail you every time.

E. The fifth field of study

Is that one Daniel and his friends were focused on – *the pursuit of the knowledge of God.* The focus will never fail you!

FAILED IN THE SERVICE
VS 7

Have you ever noticed how those involved in the service industry don't seem to be that interested in serving?

- **You go to a restaurant with more than 7 people and they automatically charge you a 20% gratuity**
- **You go to a convenience store and there is no one there to help you**
- **You order a telephone installation and they tell you what day they will come but not what time – you have to wait for them to come when they decide to come**

They say they are our servants – but they don't really want to serve us.

Nebuchadnezzar had it figured out....His "servants" would tell him just about anything he wanted to hear. But this time he did not want to hear what he wanted to hear. He wanted to hear the truth!

And they failed him.

A. They could not help king

Because they did not know the truth. That had not been their field of study.

- **They had learned to conjure up things**
- **They had learned to make things appear different than they really were**
- **They had learned to use lying spirits and evil beings**
- **They had even learned to make up some pretty good guesses (philosophy)**

But they had no clue how to get the truth.

Reminds me of a lot of religion today. They have learned to make things look

- **Good**
- **Big**
- **Successful**

But they have not learned how to get a hold of God and consequently

B. They could not save themselves

Nebuchadnezzar's demand was admittedly unreasonable. Everyone knows these guys did not have the power to tell Nebuchadnezzar what he dreamed. To threaten to hack them into pieces if they didn't tell him what his dream was is obviously cruel. But it does remind me that men are on a crash course straight to the torments of hell.

And only the fear of God and the pursuit of Him can save a soul from hell. There are plenty of people who will try to butter you up

- **I will be your friend**
- **I will make you a part of my group**
- **I will show you a good time**
- **I will keep you entertained**
- **I will not judge or condemn you**

But they can't show you how to get saved and live for God. No matter how much they tell you they are your servants – they can't help you.

FAILED IN THEIR FAITH
Vs 14-30

What I saw is that while the

- **Magicians**
- **Astrologers**

- Sorcerers
- Chaldeans

Were all about themselves and what they could and could not do; Daniel's response was completely about the Lord.

A. He desired the mercies of the God of heaven
Vs 18

- **He and his friends did not get together to come up with a plan**
- **They did not consult each other to see what wisdom they might have on their own**
- **They did not try to write an appeal to the king**

They got together for the purpose of seeking God's mercies.

I think I am as guilty of this as anybody – consulting with my preacher friends to find what their experience has taught them. Daniel and his friends had only one objective – to get in touch with the Lord. Would to God we would learn to do the same.

B. He declared the goodness of God for the answer
Vs 20

Once God had given the answer, Daniel spent personal time with the Lord giving Him honor and praise. We probably rush too much in and out of the throne room of heaven. Too many answers to prayer are never heard because we do not wait upon the Lord. Too many times God is not glorified as He ought to be because we rush out of His presence once we have what we want. There is nothing wrong with staying in the presence of God just because you want to.

C. He demanded that Nebuchadnezzar know there is a God in Heaven.
Vs 26-28

Nebuchadnezzar asked Daniel *"Art thou able..."*

Daniel's answer was not merely that the other wise men could not reveal the secret, but that he could not either. However Daniel said, *"There is a God in heaven....."* That is the only thing that really matters – that people know *there is a God in Heaven* and He can bless them and save them.
- **It does not matter that they know what we know**
- **It does not matter that they think well of us**
- **It does not matter that they tell others what we did for them**

It does matter that the world knows *there is a God in heaven*.

MAN'S KINGDOMS CRUMBLE

Daniel 2:31-45

What we have before us is most likely the most important prophetical statement in the Bible. It is important for two reasons that I know of: first, because of what it teaches. The majority of the prophetic part of the book of Daniel will be an expansion on this prophecy; teaching the same things using different metaphors and giving greater detail

Secondly, because the vast majority of it has already come to pass. This one prophecy not only shows us what will be in the future but it also proves to us that we can trust what God says will be in the future.

This is so accurate that many of the more intellectual people have criticized it and said that Daniel could not have possibly written it. It is too accurate to have been written before the things it describes had actually occurred.

King Nebuchadnezzar, who controlled the largest part of the world of his day had had a dream that troubled him. Trouble was, when he woke up he could not remember it. When his magicians, soothsayers and other wise men could not tell him what the dream was and the interpretation of it, he intended to have them all killed.

That was until Daniel and his friends prayed. Daniel was quick to tell the king that his ability to reveal to the king what his dream was and what it meant was not because of any wisdom he had, but that there is a God in heaven. And that God had told Nebuchadnezzar *"what shall come to pass"*[7]

THE DREAM

Daniel described the king's dream like this[8]:

In the dream the king saw a huge image – a statue. It sounds to me like it may have been in a valley, because there was a huge mountain next to it and nearby. This statue was immense in size and impressive in its composition.

- **Its head was made of gold**
- **Its arms and torso were made of silver**
- **Its belly and thighs of brass**
- **Its legs of iron**

---

[7] Daniel 2:29

[8] If you don't mind I am going to add just a little of my own imagination into it – based on some of the reading I have done.

- **Its feet of iron and clay mix**

Daniel told the king that in his dream he watched as a stone was thrust from the mountain and smote – attacked the image, breaking into pieces and grinding it up until it was as dust, blown away with the wind. And then Daniel said this stone, which apparently was much smaller than the image, grew itself until it was a huge mountain that filled the earth.

THE INTERPRETATION
Vs 36
Daniel informed the king that the image represented
A. The great kingdoms of the world

The first kingdom (head of Gold) was Babylon. As great and powerful as Nebuchadnezzar was, his kingdom would not last forever. God said after him would arise another kingdom represented by the torso and arms of silver. While this kingdom would be great, it would be inferior to Nebuchadnezzar's kingdom. We now know this kingdom to be that of the Medo-Persian Empire which actually came into power during the days of Daniel and is recorded in the book of Daniel. This would be followed by a third kingdom represented as the belly and thighs of brass. This kingdom we know to be Greece, which came into power just about the end of Old Testament times under Alexander the Great.

The fourth kingdom was represented by legs of iron and finally by feet of iron and clay. We know that to be the Roman Empire. The fourth kingdom will be destroyed by *"the stone cut out without hands"* And that that stone will grow into its own kingdom that will last forever. That kingdom obviously being the kingdom of the Lord Jesus Christ.

B. Some interesting thoughts concerning the image are:
1. Each kingdom rises from the other
So that the four kingdoms complete the image. They are not each individual images, they are connected into a unit that comprises the image. Man never does do anything original. We just keep redesigning what we already have. We build on top of another's foundation. Even when we think we are going to "totally redesign the wheel" we still come up with a wheel.

2. The image grew less and less valuable while at the same time becoming harder and harder.
Each of the metals in the image is less valuable monetarily, but harder physically than the other until finally what is created is so hard it is brittle and shatters.

We never really make things better. Each generation of mankind feels like it has improved upon the generations before. But we fail to see is that each generation seems to become harder and harder to the things of God until one day we will crumble under the judgment of God.

3. The focus is all on the image, but there is something much larger in the background

I have in my mind some of those beautiful pictures of the Seattle skyscrapers with Mount Rainier in the background. It seems to me like we can focus so much on

- **The Buildings**
- **The Space Needle**
- **The Seattle skyline**

That we almost blank out in our heads what God has built. It just makes a good backdrop for man's own work.

The image
C. Stands in contrast to the mountain
Vs 45

It is like we have right there before us –

- **This is what man can do**

- This is what God can do

1. What man builds is impressive-What God builds is inspiring

While we might grow enamored with the work of man, only the work of God can truly motivate a life. Men have dreamed up religious organizations and other groups of good works. And we can be so impressed with them. But only Jesus Christ built a body (the church) that still functions just the way He designed it 2000 years ago.

2. What man builds degenerates-What God builds endures

The image was made of less valuable material, the farther along it went. God's work continues to do exactly what He designed it to do. His church is:
- Just as valuable
- Just as holy
- Just as effective today

As it was 2000 years ago.

3. What man builds will corrupt the soul-What God builds will correct the sinner

We suspect that the huge statue that Nebuchadnezzar had constructed in Daniel 3 was inspired by his dream in chapter 2. The purpose of His image was that people would worship it. Most of you know the story; Shadrach, Meshech and Abednego refused to do that. But God cut the stone out of the mountain and it destroyed the image of chapter 2.

Man creates things that corrupt people and drive them away from true worship. God brought Jesus Christ to this earth to correct our sin and turn us to righteousness.

4. What man builds will blow away- What God builds will grind it to powder
Vs 35

By the time God got done with the kingdoms of man in Daniel two, they were ground to pieces and blew away like the chaff. But the kingdom that grew out of the stone – Jesus Christ, the Bible says, will stand forever (vs 44).

THE APPLICATION

A. The dream of Nebuchadnezzar in chapter two speaks of 5 literal kingdoms God says will rule on this earth.
- **The kingdom of Babylon**
- **The kingdom of the Medes and the Persians**
- **The kingdom of Greece**

- **The kingdom of Rome**
- **The kingdom of God**

Three of these kingdoms have come and gone. The Roman Empire exists still today (and rule the majority of the known world). The kingdom of God is yet to come.

I am thinking that,

B. On a somewhat smaller scale men are building other kingdoms.

- **For some – it is the kingdom of family – and you place it over God**
- **For some it is the kingdom of money – and you have no greater priority than to earn and spend.**
- **For some it is the kingdom of materialism- and you are constructing a huge image of gold and silver and less valuable goods into an image that you think speaks of your great worth**
- **For another it is the kingdom of self – and you would never consider letting God tell you how to live your life**

May I remind you what the Bible says about the things of this world?
2 Peter 3:10-12
But the day of the Lord will come as a thief in the night; in the which the heavens shall pass away with a great noise, and the elements shall melt with fervent heat, the earth also and the works that are therein shall be burned up.

Seeing then that all these things shall be dissolved, what manner of persons ought ye to be in all holy conversation and godliness,
Looking for and hasting unto the coming of the day of God, wherein the heavens being on fire shall be dissolved, and the elements shall melt with fervent heat? (KJV)

That what will happen to all the things we build
- **When we build our families**
- **When we build our reputations**
- **When we build our lives**
- **When we build our worth**

- **In the power of our flesh**
- **In disobedience to the Lord**

It is a sure thing, the Lord will grind them to powder.

C. On the other hand
- **We could let the Lord build our family**
- **We could let the Lord build our character**
- **We could let the Lord build our career**

And when we do that – then it will not only stand but flourish and grow and be a blessing, throughout the world (missions and helping preachers.)

CERTAIN MEN STANDING

Daniel 3:1-25

God had given Israel a test many years previous to this to determine if a prophet was from God or not.

- **If his prophecies came true 100% of the time, listen to him. He is from God.**
- **If his prophecies came true only a part of the time, he is a false prophet. Kill him.[9]**

I once listened to an interview of The Amazing Kreskin. He said that during his show in Seattle, he would leave the room and have his fee hidden somewhere in the theatre among the audience…If he could not find it within a certain length of time, he would forfeit the fee – the show would be free. He said he has only failed to find the check a handful of times – one time he lost $50,000. God would call him a false prophet. Good thing we don't still live in the Old Testament – he would be stoned for such a failure!

The book of Daniel predicted the future of the empires of the world so accurately that there have been so called scholars who have

---

[9] Deuteronomy 18:20-22

denied that this book could have been written by Daniel – it is too accurate. More than ¾ of the prophecies found in the book of Daniel have come to pass exactly as Daniel predicted they would. That gives us two lessons.

- **First, we can expect the rest of it to be fulfilled exactly as Daniel says.**
- **Secondly, if the prophecies are true, then so is the rest of the Bible and you and I can trust it and we would do well to obey it.**

Besides the prophetical message of the book of Daniel, there is a power message concerning the kind of character a Christian ought to have that streams throughout this book. Most of that character is revealed through the life of Daniel himself.

This chapter teaches us character lessons, not through Daniel, but through his friends, Shadrach, Meshach, and Abednego. While they occupy less space in the Bible than Daniel or some other famous figures, their life story is no less powerful.

The Bible says that when the King had finished his statue and when he had commanded everyone to bow and worship the statue, there were certain Jews who would not do so.

- **Shadrach**
- **Meshach**
- **Abednego**

Their story is one of the most well known in all of the Bible. These three Hebrews just could not worship this false god.

- **Regardless of the cost**
- **Regardless of the sacrifice**

They worshiped the true and living God and they refused to do anything else. Their sacrifice was enormous but God blessed them with something even greater – His presence

Their stand was

AN OBVIOUS STAND
Vs 4-7

Notice the words in verse 4, "...*people, nations and languages,*" This is everybody.

- **It did not matter what their background was**
- **It did not matter what their religious preferences were**
- **It did not matter if they agreed with the image or not**

The command was everyone was supposed to fall down and worship when the music started. Verse 7 says, "...*all the people, the nations, and the languages, fell down and worshipped....*"

All that is but these certain Jews. There have been a handful of times since I have become a Christian where I was forced to stand out in the group.

Over the years I have learned what types of events will most likely put me in that position and I do my best not to go to them. I don't visit other types of churches with my friends, because often those churches will do something that I can't participate in – and I stick out. It is obvious I am the only one not doing what everyone else is doing. I don't go to ecumenical types of gatherings where people from all sorts of denominations are cooperating together for some greater cause – because invariably they will want to do something I find is offensive to the Word of God and while they want me to put aside my convictions for their greater good, they would not consider putting aside their worldly practices in order to work with me.

I try to avoid functions where I am going to stick out like a sore thumb. But sometimes you just can't avoid them. You can't avoid going to work where you might be the only believer on the job. Sometimes you just can't avoid being in one of those places where you might be forced to make a stand and you are the only one making that stand.

- **Where you are the only one not drinking alcohol**
- **Where you are the only one not laughing at the dirty joke**

- Where you are the only one not dressed immodestly
- Where you are the only one not enjoying the music
- Where you are the only one not looking at a filthy magazine
- When you are the only one not voting for the liberal candidate
- When you are the only one not supporting a socialist agenda

Or on the other side of the coin;
- Were you are the only one reading a Bible
- Were you are the only one telling people about Jesus
- Were you are the only one praying before eating your meal

Even when taking a stand for what is right makes you stand out of the crowd- Shadrach Meshach and Abednego would tell you to take the stand anyway. Everyone else fell down at the king's command and there stood Shadrach, Meshach and Abednego.

Their stand was also
A LONELY STAND
The way I picture this scene, there are millions of people together in the plain of Dura. Music is playing and crowds are gathered. In the middle of this crowd Shadrach, Meshach and Abednego stand alone.

You know as well as I do, you can be surrounded by people and still be lonely. And I want to warn you – the closer you get to God, the more lonely you will become. I tend to think of loneliness as a good thing, not a bad thing. Most of us never really get to know what it means to fellowship with God because our lives are too crowded with people.

- **We have friends to occupy our time**
- **We have counselors to help us solve our questions**
- **We have activities to help us relieve our stresses**

Frankly, we seldom are quiet long enough to hear from our Heavenly Father.

I am reminded again of a story I read in a missionary book a little while back. This missionary was in the jungles of Papua New Guinea preparing to make first contact with a cannibalistic tribe. He was sleeping in a tree over night so as not to be attacked and killed in his sleep. In the middle of the night he woke as the cannibals came to get him. Breathing as quietly as he could, he could hear them searching for him under the tree. He testified that he had never experienced the presence of God like he did that night in the tree. And then he said that he would gladly go back to that frightful, lonely night, if only he could sense God's presence like that again.

Living for God is a lonely place and you will never know God's presence until you are willing to be all alone with God.

Their stand was
A DANGEROUS STAND
Vs 6

They knew exactly what the price of standing there was. They were risking going to the flames. They knew God could save them from the furnace.

- He could make it so no one noticed that they were still standing
- He could soften the king's heart so he did not care that they were standing
- He could kill the men who were going to tell the king that they were standing before they told him

Or not.

One of the hardest lessons to understand in the Bible is that God doesn't do everyone the same.

- He let Herod lop off Apostle James head but
- He sent an angel to rescue Peter from the very same jail cell James was in

- Stephen was stoned to death but
- Paul survived being stoned
- Jonathan loved David
- But God allowed him to die with his father, King Saul anyway

- Abel offered to God a pleasing sacrifice but
- God still allowed Cain to murder him

- God heals some people of cancer but
- God lets others die of it

- Missionary to China J Oscar Wells and his wife and daughter spent WWII in a Japanese prisoner of war ship
- Missionary to China John Stam and his wife, Betty were beheaded in the Boxer rebellion

If we are going to stand for God we are going to have to decide to do it regardless of our fate. God will bless some who stand with:
- Great ministries
- Super promotions
- Large numbers of souls saved

Some will see God intervene on their behalf in miraculous ways. Others will pay the price for standing for God.
- They will lose jobs
- They will lose marriages
- They will lose money
- They will lose their children

Shadrach, Meshach and Abednego understood full well the dangers of their stand. Daniel 3:16-18

Shadrach, Meshach, and Abednego, answered and said to the king, O Nebuchadnezzar, we are not careful to answer thee in this matter.

If it be so, our God whom we serve is able to deliver us from the burning fiery furnace, and he will deliver us out of thine hand, O king.
But if not, be it known unto thee, O king, that we will not serve thy gods, nor worship the golden image which thou hast set up. (KJV)

- God could deliver them or
- God might not deliver them

That made no difference to them concerning their decision.

Their stand was
AN IMPORTANT STAND
Vs 28

There are some things more important than our lives or our comfort; the truth of God's Word for one. We are living in a terrifying day:
- **Abortion is accepted as birth control**
- **Homosexuality is regarded as honorable and marriage**
- **Islam is rewarded in our country even though they are undeniably guilty of killing thousands of Americans at the Twin Towers**
- **Crime is on the rise, but parents still are told not to discipline their children**

May I tell you why this is? It is because most Christians today would have bowed along with everyone else in the plain of Dura.

- **Churches compromise with the Word of God**
- **Churches excuse sin**

Christians refuse to stand for what is right but bend the truth to do things that make them feel better about themselves. The Word of God has become relative; we know what it says, but there are ways to interpret it that fits better into what is comfortable with what we already want to do.

The Word of God is important to me. I am not going to bend to pressures to change what the Bible says just because somebody might leave the church because of it.

Shadrach, Meshach, and Abednego realized that worshiping this false god was more than just bowing down. It would have destroyed their testimony for the Lord. And because they took a stand – Nebuchadnezzar came to know the true and living God.

Their stand was:
A REWARDED STAND
Vs 23-25

A. Their ropes fell off

There is liberty in standing for right. This world will bind you with their mold:

- **They want you to think a certain way**
- **They want you to act a certain way**
- **They want you to do as they do**
- **They want you to be their puppets**

People pull you a hundreds different ways:

- **This is what they feel you should do**
- **This is what they think you should do**
- **Here is what most people would do**
- **Here is what Dr Phil and Oprah say to do**

And you are pulled all these different ways….Until you decide you are going to stand for God….. And the ropes burn off.

There is freedom in living to please only the Lord.

B. They walked with God

I don't know if I would have listened to Nebuchadnezzar tell them to come out of the flames. I can't imagine anything better than being in the middle of the fire, God walking with me! They didn't get burned; they didn't even smell like smoke.

C. They changed Nebuchadnezzar's mind about God
And someone needs to do that to our world leaders today. We have these:

- **Mealy mouthed**
- **Liberal thinking**
- **Crowd pleasing**
- **Compromising**

ministers that offer counsel and spiritual guidance to what few leaders will even listen to some spiritual word. Oh for someone who will stand up for what is true!

- **Who will not bow to this world's pressures**
- **Who will go out to**
  - **Neighbors**
  - **Workmates**
  - **Family**
  - **Friends**
  - **Whomever else God gives them opportunity to speak to**

and tell them what is the truth of the Word of God?

NEBUCHADNEZZAR'S GONE NUTS

Daniel 4:1-18

I have said that the book of Daniel has two main focuses:
- **One – prophetical**
- **The second one – concerning character**

Character is taught from a couple of difference perspectives. **We can learn from good examples**. God's Word sets up one man after the other as heroes for our walk of faith.
- **Enoch; who walked with God and was not for God took him**
- **Abraham; believed God and it was accounted unto him for righteousness**
- **Joseph; who refused to grow bitter despite one hardship after the other**
- **Moses: rebounded from defeat to become one of the greatest leaders of all time**
- **David a man with a heart after God**

Hebrews chapter twelve provides example after example of men and women of faith. So as we study the Word of God, we have these and many other positive examples of character. But perhaps we learn the best from negative examples. Haven't you noticed how children learn best from negative situations rather than the positive ones?

89

"Nancy New Mommy" and her husband "Ned New Daddy" have taken pre-parenting classes at the local community college. In the course they were taught all the tools of positive reinforcement:

- **Reward you child for good behavior**
- **Recognize your child's gifts**
- **Remind your child he is precious**

and never, never, never damage your child's spirit by telling them they are bad. Nine months comes along and they are delivered with their brand new baby, "Suzie Sweetie". Nancy and Ned don't want to hurt Suzie's delicate soul so,

- **They excuse her temper tantrums as an infant**
- **They defend her biting in the nursery when she is a toddler**
- **They pamper her fits when she hits preschool**

And Suzie Sweetie has transformed into Mary Monster by the time she is 10.

On the other hand, "Christy Christian Mom" and her husband, "Bob Bible Believer" read the Word of God. They figured out early that their child would be born with a sin nature just like everyone else and they determined to use the Word of God rather than modern philosophy to bring up their child. No sooner did they get their new bundle of joy, "Billy Blessed Home" than did they begin to teach him what the word "no" means.

Billy's parents love him intensely, but they wouldn't let him get away with sinfulness. And by the time Billy was 10 years old – people in the restaurants enjoyed Billy and complimented his behavior but finished their meals early and got out quickly when Suzie came in. Sure – children whose lessons are reinforced with a switch to the back side learn their lessons more quickly than do those whose parents never get negative with their kids (if those kids ever learn.)

So God uses not only positive role models in the Word of God but negative ones as well to train us in character.

Daniel chapter four deals with the chastisement of a particular sin – pride. I want to treat more God's dealing with the sin than the particular sin itself. I find in here a process we may expect the Lord to put us through in dealing with our own sins.

THERE WAS A WARNING
Vs 20-26

In Nebuchadnezzar's case the warning was the dream and the interpreter of it. In our case – we have the Word of God and the preacher of it.

I read in my Bible that the word of God is called *"the word of His grace."* The Bible is a book full of grace.

- It was a gracious thing that God gave it to us
- It is a gracious thing that it tells us how to be saved
- It is a gracious thing that it describes for us some of what heaven will be like
- It is a gracious thing that the Bible tells about rewards for faithfulness to the things of God

- But it is also a gracious thing that the Bible warns us about hell
- And it is also a gracious thing that the Bible describes for us the Tribulation
- And it is a gracious thing that the Bible says we all come short of the glory of God
- And it is a gracious thing that the Bible tells us we deserve to go to hell

- It is a word of Grace to learn how God parted the Red Sea for Israel
- But it is also his grace that caused Him to tell how Pharaoh hardened his heart and he and his soldiers were drowned in the same Red Sea

The doctor who tells you that you have cancer does so out of grace. For God to confront you and me through a man of God and warn us concerning our sin is an act of grace and love. Daniel heard the dream and the Bible says he was *"astonied for one hour and his thoughts troubled him."* Vs 19 He could have been the other way

- "You took me into slavery and I am glad you are going to get it."
- "You made the golden image and caused people to worship and I am glad God is going to get you."
- "You are a vile heathen king and I am glad your getting yours."

That was not Daniel's attitude at all. His was a reaction of genuine care for the king! There was a warning. "King, God has determined to judge your sin."

THERE WAS AN ANSWER
Vs 27

I want to make a statement that some might not quite appreciate; God is always willing to repent, if we will repent. God is always willing to stop the judgment He has determined upon us if we will *"break off our sins by righteousness."*

A. The first thing that comes to my mind when I see that phrase *"by righteousness"* is

Matthew 5:20

For I say unto you, That except your righteousness shall exceed the righteousness of the scribes and Pharisees, ye shall in no case enter into the kingdom of heaven. (KJV)

The righteousness God expects of us is far greater than we can ever obtain. When a man is as righteous as He can possibly be, the Bible still says of him

Isaiah 64:6

But we are all as an unclean thing, and all our righteousnesses are as filthy rags; and we all do fade as a leaf; and our iniquities, like the wind, have taken us away. (KJV)

Praise the Lord I don't have to approach God with my own righteousness.

2 Corinthians 5:21

For he hath made him to be sin for us, who knew no sin; that we might be made the righteousness of God in him. (KJV)

Jesus offers me His very own righteousness and it is available, according to the Abraham's account simply for the believing.....

Romans 4:3

For what saith the scripture? Abraham believed God, and it was counted unto him for righteousness. (KJV)

If a person is lost in sin – unsaved all they need do is
- **Believe that Jesus died for their sins**
- **Call upon His name**
- **Jesus will apply His own righteousness to our lives**

B. But what about the person who is saved but sinning?
Two things
1. I John 1:9
If we confess our sins, he is faithful and just to forgive us our sins, and to cleanse us from all unrighteousness. (KJV)

When you are confronted with your sins
- **From the Word of God**
- **From the man of God**

Confess it.
- **Don't get offended**
- **Don't start excusing yourself**
- **Don't start blaming someone else**

Confess your sin.

2. Titus 2:12-13
Teaching us that, denying ungodliness and worldly lusts, we should live soberly, righteously, and godly, in this present world;

Looking for that blessed hope, and the glorious appearing of the great God and our Saviour Jesus Christ; (KJV)

Then turn from it. Jesus told the woman taken in adultery, *"Neither do I condemn thee; go, and sin no more."*

A pardon from the Lord is not an excuse to keep sinning.
- **Deny ungodliness and worldly lust in your life**
- **Live soberly, righteously and godly in this present world**

THERE WAS A PAUSE BEFORE JUDGMENT
Vs 29

It was a full year between when Nebuchadnezzar had the dream and when the judgment began. We have to be very careful not to interpret God's patience with God being slack.

Years ago I lived in a 33 foot travel trailer with three rodeo buddies and my dog, Shedrow. I wasn't using very good sense back then and I allowed these other three to move in even though none of them had jobs but me.
- **I was making payments on the trailer**
- **I was making payments on the trailer space**
- **I was paying all of the utility bills**

- **I was buying all of the food for us all**

I did it because I thought it was cool to have this rodeo crowd around me all of the time. I thought we were friends but really I was just being used. One of the guys, Nick Beeler, knew a girl, I think she was in Alaska. Without my knowing it and during the peak daytime hours, Nick was making long distance calls to her on the phone I was paying for. I only found out about it when the Telephone Company called me at work to ask me what was going on.

I have to tell you I absolutely went berserk! I called my house and told Don and Nick to get out before I got home. That was a mistake. They did it and I never got a chance to try to get money from them.

- **I had a right, I believed, to be very upset**
- **I had a right, I believed, to want to whip Nick Beeler**
- **I had every intention of doing just that**

But it took me several months to find him. Over the course of time my wrath began to dwindle. One day I was driving down 10th Street in Pasco, WA and there was Nick, walking down the sidewalk. I pulled my pickup over and got out, planning on thumping him but Nick was one of those guys who could talk himself out of situations. And to be honest with you, by that time I had already paid off the Telephone bill. I just wasn't mad enough to fight him.

Some of us think God is like that.

- **If I get away with my sin today**
- **If I get away with it tomorrow**
- **If I get away with it long enough**

God probably won't get me at all. That is not true! Don't interpret God's grace in giving you more time to repent as God winking at your sin.

THERE WAS A PUNISHMENT
Vs 30-33

A. Judgment came just as prophesied
God's Word is careful to describe it so that we see what happened to Nebuchadnezzar was exactly like God said it would be.

- **God's Word describes the judgment of hell and the Lake of Fire**
- **God's Word describes the judgment of the terrible Tribulation**
- **God's Word describes the Great White Throne judgment**
- **God's Word describes the judgment seat of Christ**
- **God's Word describes a chastening of His children**

I am going to tell you; they will be just exactly like God's Word describes them.

B. Judgment came surely

It may have been twelve months later. But twelve months goes by very fast. It may seem like His judgments don't come when we expect them but they will come surely and when they come – we will think they came suddenly.

THERE WAS A RESTORATION
Vs 34-37

Now unfortunately the Word of God very clearly tells us that those who refuse to get saved and go into the Tribulation judgment will have no second chance to get saved. And the Bible is very clear that the man who goes to Hell will end up suffering there for ever and ever. There is no hope to escape.

But in every other case of judgment, there is hope to be restored. Just as Nebuchadnezzar was out of his mind. So is the person who is caught up in sin and won't confess and forsake it.

God graciously gave Nebuchadnezzar the chance to get things right. After seven years of insanity, God cleared his mind and let him see Jesus.

My Great Grandfather Baker was out of his mind as far back as I can remember. But I do know that he had lived a worldly life, earning his living by owning bars and taverns. He and Nana Baker lived in Longview, WA. Not too far from Anita and I when I was the pastor of Bayview Baptist Church there. Despite his senility, Nana and Grandpa lived in their own home until they were well into their 90's. But then Nana Baker fell and broke her hip which necessitated the two of them going to a nursing home.

They never left there. My Grandpa called me one day and told me that Grandpa Baker was in pretty bad shape and said I ought to go visit him if I wanted to see him before he died. I went into the room to see him curled in the fetal position rocking back and forth and crying

- **Pain**
- **Pain**
- **Pain**

I do not ever remember conversing with Grandpa Baker so I visited with Nana while I watched Grandpa rock back and forth;

- **Pain**
- **Pain**
- **Pain**

As I left the room I asked the nurse at the desk if she could do something for his pain and she said no. She said that his heart was swollen and that he should be dead. But she said, for some reason he is fighting death. I drove home that night heartbroken. The next day I determined to go back and give Grandpa Baker the plan of salvation. Someone had told me that sometimes people can hear you even when they can't respond to you and I wanted to tell him about the Lord hoping that he might be able to hear.

There he was still in the fetal position
- **Pain**
- **Pain**
- **Pain**

I took his hand in mind and I went through the plan of salvation. Then I prayed the sinner's prayer and asked my great grandfather, "Grandpa, if you could understand and if you prayed for Jesus to save you just now, would you squeeze my hand?" Grandpa, for the first time since I had taken his hand squeezed long and hard. Then he relaxed. He laid down straight in his bed. He stopped crying "Pain pain pain". And he died a few hours later. I believe God cleared his mind and let him meet Jesus.

Sometimes when we find ourselves in the midst of chastening
- **We feel like there is no hope**
- **We feel like we have offended God to the place He will never loves us a gain and never bless us again**

But Nebuchadnezzar's story tells us that there is always hope

- **Two years down the road**
- **Three years down the road**
- **Four years down the road even**
- **Seven years down the road (the number of completion – could represent a lifetime)**

Still, when he lifted up his eyes unto Heaven God restored him.

- **There is a warning against sin**
- **There is an answer for sin**
- **There is often a pause before judgment**
- **There is a punishment for sin but**
- **There is always hope of restoration**

It would be best to heed God's warning and get things right before the judgment comes. But if it is too late for that, if you know that God is judging you right now, it is never too late to lift up your eyes to the Lord and let Him restore you.

THE PARTY'S OVER

Daniel 5:1-6

One of the things that is obvious about the Bible is that it is brutally true. There are many wonderful and precious promises in the Word of God. But God's Word never whitewashes the human condition or the consequences of it.

Daniel chapter five contains the story of a young man who had everything in the world in his favor.

- **He was wealthy**
- **He was powerful**
- **He was the child of one who had heard of the living God**

The Bible says that Belshazzar's father was Nebuchadnezzar but most of the commentaries say that he was really his grandfather and that he co-ruled with his father, Nabonidus, who was away fighting the Medes and Persians while Belshazzar served as Viceroy in Babylon.

Belshazzar had without doubt heard the stories of Nebuchadnezzar's experiences. It is pretty difficult to read Nebuchadnezzar's declaration in Daniel 4:34-37 and not come to the conclusion that he would have told everyone he came into contact with who God is.

Nebuchadnezzar would not have been limited by the insecurities that limit us.

- **He was naturally a confident and competent world leader**
- **He controlled the biggest part of the known world**

- **There is no one who is not going to listen to his testimony**
- **There is no question about his testimony**

So you just know that Belshazzar has heard the stories of his grandfather's relationship with God.

It is not surprising that Belshazzar would have ignored that testimony. Young people do it every day.

- **A man gets saved and his life is turned around**
- **He raises his children in an entirely different way than he was raised; protecting them from the things that almost destroyed him**

Yet time and time again I have witnessed those children turn from the faith of their fathers.

I know preachers whose hearts are broken.

- **Because their children have ignored their urgings to live for the Lord and**

- Because their grandchildren practically act as if they had no idea who God is

A man devotes his life to telling people about the Lord and encouraging them to turn to Christ only to have his very own children and grandchildren turn their backs upon the God he loves.

Belshazzar had everything in this world going for him but in one night his revelry turns into:
- **Terror**
- **Defeat**
- **Death**

Here is the scene. While his father was out fighting the enemy Belshazzar was placed in charge of the city. A city that was considered impenetrable. Though the Medes and Persians had laid siege to Babylon, it was not considered a real threat. So Belshazzar,
- **Probably as a slap in the face of the enemy**
- **But also maybe to bolster the confidence of his citizens**

planned his party. There they were:
- **Surrounded by an enemy**
- **Their armies out fighting to save their lives**

And they are inside partying.

This reminds me a lot of what people are like today. The signs of the times point to the soon return of Jesus Christ.

- **Evil is waxing worse and worse**
- **Homosexuality and other forms of perversion are taken for granted**

Even the lost world recognizes that these things point to the end of time as we know it. Movies and books like the *Left Behind* series are more popular than any time in history. But the world still just goes happily partying away, unaware or else unconcerned about the dangers of the Tribulation and Hell.

Belshazzar and his friends began to drink and party and things got more and more carried away until he ordered that the vessels of God's house be brought in. Rather than slapping the face of the Medes and the Persians, Belshazzar practically slaps the face of Almighty God.

As we approach the end of the world as we know, it we find the same thing happening. This wicked world, growing in the confidence of their wickedness, is not just content to be wicked, but it seems like, is blaspheming the things of God.

So called churches who use the world's wicked music. So called Christians who live more like the devil than the Lord.

- **We have Christian athletes**
- **We have Christian actors and actresses**
- **We have Christian celebrities**
- **We even have Christian mobsters and Christian strippers**

Just about anything can be done in the name of the Lord these days and nearly everybody will claim it is all right.

But it is not all right.

Belshazzar believed he could carry on with his wickedness just like he mostly had done many times in the past, and nothing really bad would happen.

But not that night.

All of a sudden the party was silent as the hand of God appeared and just as suddenly disappeared, but left the writing on the wall. The Bible says,

- **His countenance was changed**
- **His thoughts troubled him**
- **His knees smote one against another**

The party was over.

I am convinced that there comes a time in every man's life

- **When we see the handwriting on the wall**
- **When the party of our life comes to a screeching halt**
- **When we are confronted in our soul with our sins**

Belshazzar did just like most of us would do

- **He called all the worldly counselors in to help him out**

But they could not do it so

- **Daniel was called in**

In Belshazzar's case, it sounds like he didn't even know who Daniel was. When Daniel came he couldn't really help Belshazzar get things right with God – it was too late for that.

And that is the way it is with some people. By the time they come to the preacher, their problem is really past fixing......

Daniel pronounced the judgment

Daniel 5:18-23

O thou king, the most high God gave Nebuchadnezzar thy father a kingdom, and majesty, and glory, and honour:

And for the majesty that he gave him, all people, nations, and languages, trembled and feared before him: whom he would he slew; and whom he would he kept alive; and whom he would he set up; and whom he would he put down.

But when his heart was lifted up, and his mind hardened in pride, he was deposed from his kingly throne, and they took his glory from him:

And he was driven from the sons of men; and his heart was made like the beasts, and his dwelling was with the wild asses: they fed him with grass like oxen, and his body was wet with the dew of heaven; till he knew that the most high God ruled in the kingdom of men, and that he appointeth over it whomsoever he will.

And thou his son, O Belshazzar, hast not humbled thine heart, though thou knewest all this;

But hast lifted up thyself against the Lord of heaven; and they have brought the vessels of his house before thee, and thou, and thy lords, thy wives, and thy concubines, have drunk wine in them; and thou hast praised the gods of silver, and gold, of brass, iron, wood, and stone, which see not, nor hear, nor know: and the God in whose hand thy breath is, and whose are all thy ways, hast thou not glorified: (KJV)

Daniel 5:25-28

And this is the writing that was written, MENE, MENE, TEKEL, UPHARSIN.

This is the interpretation of the thing: MENE; God hath numbered thy kingdom, and finished it.

TEKEL; Thou art weighed in the balances, and art found wanting.

PERES; Thy kingdom is divided, and given to the Medes and Persians. (KJV)

The Bible tells us that there is coming a day when God will say just about the same thing to this world.

Revelation 14:10

109

The same shall drink of the wine of the wrath of God, which is poured out without mixture into the cup of his indignation; and he shall be tormented with fire and brimstone in the presence of the holy angels, and in the presence of the Lamb: (KJV)

That very night the Medes gained entrance into the city and took it almost without a battle. One description goes like this,

The army of the Medes and Persians was camped near the Euphrates River. Historians tell us that Babylon fell to the Medes and the Persians in a surprise attack. The army managed to divert the river into a nearby lake. With the river dried up, the way was open into the city. One ancient writer even says that when the army entered the city, they found the Babylonians feasting in a time of drunken revelry. Not long after Daniel gave his solemn message to the king. The Medo-Persian army entered Babylon almost without a fight. Before sunrise Belshazzar was dead and the Babylonian Empire came to an inglorious end.[10]

GOD'S WORD IS SURE

There are at least two fulfilled prophecies in this chapter:

A. That Babylon would fall

Daniel had told Nebuchadnezzar that would happen something like 50 years previous to this when the king had the dream of the image of

---

[10] http://www.calvarymemorial.com/sermons/SMdisplay.asp?id=64, accessed 5-5-06

- Gold
- Silver
- Brass
- Iron
- Clay

Daniel had told him that the Gold head of the image represented Babylon but that it would be overcome by another kingdom. Both Isaiah and Jeremiah prophesied years and years before it came to pass describing the means by which the city would be taken and even that it would be the Medes who took it.

Jeremiah 51:53-58

Though Babylon should mount up to heaven, and though she should fortify the height of her strength, yet from me shall spoilers come unto her, saith the LORD.

A sound of a cry cometh from Babylon, and great destruction from the land of the Chaldeans:

Because the LORD hath spoiled Babylon, and destroyed out of her the great voice; when her waves do roar like great waters, a noise of their voice is uttered:

Because the spoiler is come upon her, even upon Babylon, and her mighty men are taken, every one of their bows is broken: for the LORD God of recompences shall surely requite.

And I will make drunk her princes, and her wise men, her captains, and her rulers, and her mighty men: and they shall sleep a perpetual sleep, and not wake, saith the King, whose name is the LORD of hosts.

Thus saith the LORD of hosts; The broad walls of Babylon shall be utterly broken, and her high gates shall be burned with fire; and the people shall labour in vain, and the folk in the fire, and they shall be weary. (KJV)

Isaiah 45:1-3

Thus saith the LORD to his anointed, to Cyrus, whose right hand I have holden, to subdue nations before him; and I will loose the loins of kings, to open before him the two leaved gates; and the gates shall not be shut;
I will go before thee, and make the crooked places straight: I will break in pieces the gates of brass, and cut in sunder the bars of iron:
And I will give thee the treasures of darkness, and hidden riches of secret places, that thou mayest know that I, the LORD, which call thee by thy name, am the God of Israel. (KJV)

Isaiah 13:17-19

Behold, I will stir up the Medes against them, which shall not regard silver; and as for gold, they shall not delight in it.
Their bows also shall dash the young men to pieces; and they shall have no pity on the fruit of the womb; their eye shall not spare children.
And Babylon, the glory of kingdoms, the beauty of the Chaldees' excellency, shall be as when God overthrew Sodom and Gomorrah. (KJV)

God's Word is sure which means

- We need to know our Bibles
- We need to believe our Bibles
- We need to obey our Bibles

GOD WEIGHS EVERY HUMAN HEART

Belshazzar isn't the only one whose life the Lord searches.

Genesis 6:5

And GOD saw that the wickedness of man was great in the earth, and that every imagination of the thoughts of his heart was only evil continually. (KJV)

Genesis 18:20-21

And the LORD said, Because the cry of Sodom and Gomorrah is great, and because their sin is very grievous;
I will go down now, and see whether they have done altogether according to the cry of it, which is come unto me; and if not, I will know.
(KJV)

Job 1:8

And the LORD said unto Satan, Hast thou considered my servant Job, that there is none like him in the earth, a perfect and an upright man, one that feareth God, and escheweth evil? (KJV)

Since he suggested that Satan consider Job, I get the impression God had already considered him.

Proverbs 15:3

The eyes of the LORD are in every place, beholding the evil and the good.
(KJV)

Belshazzar was accountable for the light he had. God had provided him opportunity to know right and wrong and God help him accountable for what he did with that knowledge.

So God inspects your life and mine.

GOD WILL NOT STRIVE WITH MAN FOREVER
Genesis 6:3
And the LORD said, My spirit shall not always strive with man, for that he also is flesh: yet his days shall be an hundred and twenty years. (KJV)

Sinners like to believe they can continue in a life of ever increasing sin without consequence or judgment. Or else we like to think that if judgment is coming, we have still have time to make it right later. That just is not true. There is going to come a day when the hand of God works suddenly and swiftly. There will be:
- **No time to consider the hour**
- **No time to recognize that time has run out**
- **No time to make those last minute confessions**

Years ago I was crossing the Young's River Bridge between Astoria and Warrenton, Oregon. Some months previous a member of our church, Brother George Braunschweiger had been killed in a traffic accident on that bridge. As I was crossing I met a log truck that lost a piece of bark and hit my windshield just about face level. I remember seeing it just before it hit and ducking just as it hit. Since it was only a piece of bark, it shattered and my car and I were fine. But I thought to myself right then – if that had been a log slipped off, I would have been dead exactly as fast as that bark hit my car.

- **No time to say goodbye to my family**
- **No time to say one last prayer to God**
- **No time to make things right for eternity**

If that had been something more substantial, the party would be over.

Some of us live our lives like it is one big party.

- **We do not think about the consequences of our actions**
- **We do not try to make things right with almighty God**
- **We only care about making tomorrow more exciting and fun than today**

But one day, for every one of us, the party will be over. We have to ask ourselves the question; If that day were today, would we be ready?

THE DECEIVERS

Daniel 6:1-9; 11-15; 24

Daniel chapter 6 is maybe the most familiar chapter of this book and probably the one of the most familiar in the entire Bible. It is the story of Daniel in the den of lions. (Not the lion's den – a lion's den might be empty of lions. This den had lions in it!) Every Sunday school kid learns this lesson a dozen times between nursery and teen class.

I have found three significant characters that make up the story:
- **Darius the king**
- **Daniel the man of prayer**
- **Deceivers, princes and presidents**

I want to begin with the last on my list first. Notice first, the deceiver's

PLOT
Vs 1-9

King Darius, in order to establish a system of command, had set up

- **Three presidents**
- **One hundred twenty princes**

Daniel
Was the first of the presidents
Vs 2
Was preferred above the others
Vs 3
He was an authority over them, but they were authorities too.

Every one of us have our own places of
- **Leadership**
- **Influence**
- **Authority**

We spoil what God could do with us whenever we get jealous of those
- **Whose authority is above ours**
- **Are preferred before us**

In verse 4 they sought an occasion against him. God's leaders can expect opposition.

There seems to always be someone who seeks to find something to use against you. But they could find no fault in him. So they developed a plot. They had, through searching Daniel's life, seen that he was a devoted believer in his God.

In verse 5 they said, "If we are going to trip Daniel at all, it will have to be by his faith." The world has no problem blaspheming our faith and denying our God. Daniel was predictable. These deceivers knew enough about Daniel to know that he would be faithful to his God even if the law said not to be.

They came to the king in verses 6-8.
A. They used majority influence
"...we have consulted together....

Majority rule is not always good rule. Our country is a good example. Evil men have banded together to use majority rule to cause evil things to become laws. Nearly every time majority rule is found in the Bible it is seen in a bad light.

B. They used flattery
No one should worship any god but you O king!

Whenever someone flatters you, be careful. Paul warned about wolves in sheep's clothing; those who want to destroy you often times will appear to be the nicest people around you, but they are buttering you up for the kill.

C. They used deceit
"All the presidents... have consulted together..."

That was a lie. Daniel had not been consulted. Darius fell for the deceit and signed the irreversible decree. Be very careful about your actions. Much of what we do is in some way irreversible.
- **An unkind word**
- **An immoral activity**
- **A hateful action**

Praise the Lord we can ask His forgiveness and be forgiven of these things but we can never take away the consequences of them.

When I was young I liked to ride bulls.
- **There is nothing that is really sinful about that**
- **And when I did it I did not get hurt that badly**

Today many years after riding my last bull, I live with pain daily that all started with me riding bulls. By the grace of God we need to make sure we do things that we won't regret later – sometimes years later.

The deceivers plotted against Daniel

PERSISTENCE
Vs 11-15

Can you see them?
- As they hid in the bushes, outside Daniel's window,
- As they hired spies to do all night surveillance at Daniel's place
- As they followed him as Daniel went about the king's business

A. They knew Daniel would break this law
He was, after all, faithful to his God. They watched in unison. They knew the king would be unhappy so they wanted a multitude of witnesses.

B. They were not false witnesses in the sense that they lied about Daniel's prayer
They were false witnesses in the sense that they used the truth for an evil purpose.

It is possible to use the truth with the wrong motives and thus spoil the virtue of the truth.

When they reported Daniel's prayer to Darius in verse 14 the king was sore displeased – not with Daniel for praying, but with himself for signing the decree and for being deceived.

Think through your actions so that you do nothing you will regret later. The king spent all day trying to find a way to save Daniel from the den of lions but he could not. In all his power he could not reverse the decree. The deceivers persisted until Daniel was finally cast into the den of lions.

C. The king kept the law perfectly.

But not before comforting Daniel that he believed Daniel's God could do what Darius himself could not do and deliver him from the lions.

The deceivers
PLUNGE
Vs 24

It is an absolute truth,
A. Wickedness never prospers
Those who lie and cheat to prosper themselves will eventually be punished.

Proverbs 26:27 says
Whoso diggeth a pit shall fall therein: and he that rolleth a stone, it will return upon him. (KJV)

That is exactly what happened to these presidents and princes.

- **They were guilty of plotting against Daniel**
- **They were guilty of deceiving the king**
- **They were guilty of attempted murder of Daniel**
- **They were guilty of treason to the country**

The king sentenced them to the same fate they had falsely condemned Daniel to.

The great tragedy here is that their families suffered the same fate as they did. We may think it is unfair in this case but it does teach us this lesson. We do not sin alone. What we do will effect our families and our families' families. But these men got exactly what they deserved.

B. We who serve God are often abused by the lovers of this world

But in the end it will be the worldlings that receive the greater condemnation.

DARIUS

Daniel 6:1-3; 8-9; 14-20; 24-27

Leadership makes mistakes.

- **Leaders still have to be leaders even when they make mistakes and**
- **Those who are followers are never right to rebel against leaders just because they make mistakes.**

Last chapter we looked at Daniel chapter six with our thoughts upon the deceivers – those presidents and princes who tried to have Daniel killed. I called them "The Deceivers" There are two more characters in the chapter we want to see:

- **Darius**
- **Daniel**

Notice first
THE KING'S MISTAKE
Vs 1-3; 8-9

Wisely, Darius had taken precautions to keep wicked me from mismanaging the kingdom. He set up

- **Three presidents**
- **One hundred twenty princes**

These men were accountable to a chain of command
- **Princes to presidents**
- **Presidents to Daniel**
- **Daniel to Darius**

The king's mistake came when the deceitful presidents and princes talked Darius into signing a decree that would make it illegal for Daniel to worship his God. Darius made three major mistakes we all ought to heed.

A. Darius fell for the flattery
Vs 6-9
Don't think more highly of yourself than you ought. Flattery is a lie dressed to butter you up. Be careful!

B. Darius didn't consult Daniel
Vs 6-9
There is safety in a multitude of counselors.

C. Darius didn't think through his actions to see where they would lead.
God says we ought to count the cost before undertaking a venture. God tells us to "be not hasty" especially is that true when the results can't be changed.

THE KING'S MISERY
Vs 14-24

A. The king was terribly upset with himself

And rightly so. He knew he had done wrong. He didn't blame the deceivers until he had blamed himself. We are responsible for our own sins. We can't blame others for them.

The king's mistake had adversely affected Daniel; usually our sins hurt somebody else. When the king could find no way to deliver Daniel he was forced to keep the law. When we give our word, even when we don't like it, we are obligated to keep it.

The king cast Daniel in the den of lions; he comforted Daniel with words of faith (Christians can be comforted by the Bible) and sealed the den according to the law.

B. The king spent an entire night praying and fasting.

- He wasn't being entertained
- He wasn't watching his favorite show

Darius was keenly interested that God would save Daniel. We might see more prayers answered if we were earnest enough to stay up all night praying and fasting also. We need to learn that effective prayer costs something.

All night long Darius
- **Prayed**
- **Fasted**
- **First thing in the morning**

Darius was out to the den.

Had God spared Daniel?

Daniel 6:20-21

And when he came to the den, he cried with a lamentable voice unto Daniel: and the king spake and said to Daniel, O Daniel, servant of the living God, is thy God, whom thou servest continually, able to deliver thee from the lions?

Then said Daniel unto the king, O king, live for ever. (KJV)

Man, this was one happy king!

Daniel 6:23

Then was the king exceeding glad .... (KJV)
- **He had prayed**
- **He had received answers to his prayers**
- **He was filled with joy**

Jesus said John 16:24

....Ask and ye shall receive, that your joy may be full.

THE KING'S MESSAGE

Vs 25-27

To all people nations and languages – world rule

A. Peace be multiplied to you

If men will worship the true God the God of Daniel, they will have peace that passes understanding. This was really more than a nice gesture. Darius was going to share a message of peace.

He decrees that

B. Men should tremble and fear God

The only true peace possible is based upon the foundation of the fear of God. Until men and women fear God no peace is possible in this world.

Why fear God?

1. He is the living God

Not like the idols of Babylon.

2. His kingdom is indestructible

- **Darius had taken this kingdom from Babylon**
- **Alexander the Great would take it from Darius**
- **Nobody takes away God's kingdom**

3. He delivers, rescues, and works signs and wonders

He is an active God; alive and working in the midst of people.

Therefore
- **Those that do not fear God should**
- **Those that do fear Him will gain peace from him**

DANIEL – CREDENTIALS, CONSISTENCY, CONFESSION

Daniel 6:1-5; 10-11; 20-22; 28

Daniel 6 may be one of the most well known chapters in all of the Bible. Certainly every child who has attended Sunday school has learned the lesson of Daniel and the Den of Lions a dozen times from nursery to Teen Class.

I find three key characters in the chapter: First there are the presidents and princes. I call them **the deceivers.**

- **They plot out a way to get Daniel killed**
- **They persistently work their plot until the King is forced to cast Daniel into the Den of Lions**
- **They eventually are plunged into the same fate that they hoped to send Daniel to (cast themselves into the den of lions.)**

Secondly there is the king, **Darius**

- **He made the mistake of believing president's flattery and signing the decree that no one pray to anyone but him for 30 days**
- **He then faced the misery of keeping his word. And the sleepless night praying for Daniel**
- **He gave his message that men should fear and tremble before the living God**

The third character is obviously Daniel. I want to give you, in this chapter, Daniel's

- **Credentials**
- **Consistency**
- **Confession**

DANIEL'S CREDENTIALS
Vs 1-5

Why was he so elevated in position? Here is a man who had served under not just the last king, but the last kingdom.

- **He is not one of the Medes and Persians**
- **He is not even a Babylonian**
- **He is a Jew in a strange land**

And Darius promotes him to not just one of the three presidents who are over 120 princes.

Darius makes Daniel first among the three. It is to Daniel's credit that he was an influential man during the reigns of

- **Nebuchadnezzar**
- **Belshazzar**
- **Cyrus**
- **Darius**

Many times in those days when a new king arose he would kill all of the officers of the old king. Even today in business a new management usually replaces all of the managers with their own people. So for Daniel to be able to survive, even to thrive in the reigns of all these kings is outstanding and much to his credit.

Daniel was preferred the Bible says first.
A. Because "an excellent spirit was in him;"
Vs 3

Of course **_the_ _excellent_ _Spirit_** is the Holy Spirit of God which indwells us at salvation. If we allow Him to control us, our Spirit will be excellent too. I am convinced that the passage is not just speaking of the Holy Ghost in Daniel but of Daniel's own spirit. We are composed as a "tri-part" being
- **Body**
- **Soul**
- **Spirit**

It is possible for people to have different kinds of a spirit.

- Saul had an evil spirit that caused him to be discontented and to loose his temper easily. It also filled him with jealousy.
- Some have a peaceful spirit where little seems to bother them and they spread peace.

- Others have a joyful spirit and they seem to have joy and good cheer in the face of the worst of circumstances.

Daniel had an excellent spirit.

I think that means the Daniel demonstrated all sorts of fruit of the Spirit.

- **Love**
- **Joy**
- **Peace**
- **Longsuffering**
- **Gentleness**
- **Goodness**
- **Faith**
- **Meekness**
- **Temperance**

All of us ought to try to cultivate the best kind of spirit.

- **If we are negative**
- **If we are discontented**
- **If we are grumpy**

That spirit will keep us from being everything God wants us to be. We need to cultivate a spirit that generates the fruit of the Spirit in our lives.

One way to tell that kind of Spirit you have is by honestly evaluating the kind of atmosphere you create when you are around people. Does your presence cause a good atmosphere or a bad one?

Daniel was preferred,
B. Because there was no fault they could find in him
Vs 4

I call this the credential of integrity. He was honest. Those wicked rulers tried everything they could to find something that Daniel did wrong. But they could find none.

- **He wasn't extorting the king's money**
- **He wasn't involved in any sex scandal**
- **He hadn't taken any bribes**
- **He wasn't using his power for personal gain**

Daniel was clean.

Obviously he was also:

- **Wise**
- **Experienced**
- **So forth**

But his spirit and his integrity are singled out here as the two reasons why he prospered.

DANIEL'S CONSISTENCY
Vs 10-11

After the law had been passed that no one could ask a petition of any god or man for 30 days, Daniel did as he always did and prayed to the Lord.

A. He prayed openly
He didn't sneak around.

- **He wasn't praying to get praise of men**
- **He wasn't afraid to be caught praying either**

B. He gave thanks
That wouldn't be easy to do about that point but He gave thanks.

Don't you wish the Bible didn't say some of the things it says?

The Bible says
1Thessalonians 5:18
In every thing give thanks: for this is the will of God in Christ Jesus concerning you. (KJV)

There are days I wished that wasn't in the Bible. There are some things I would rather not give God thanks for. But God says *"In everything give thanks; for this is the will of God in Christ Jesus concerning you."*

Philippians 4:6
Be careful for nothing; but in every thing by prayer and supplication with thanksgiving let your requests be made known unto God. (KJV)

There are days when I would rather not let my requests be made known with thanksgiving. One writer said, *"Those who base their lives on the belief that a loving God is acting in their behalf tend to see problems as opportunities for growth."*

God is acting on our behalf. Let's thank him for that.

C. He did nothing differently
"...as he did aforetime."

Daniel did not begin his prayer vigil because of the decree. His prayer was not a simple demonstration of civil disobedience. He just did what he had been doing probably for the past 70 years.

Three times a day:

- He went to his house
- Opened the windows toward Jerusalem
- Prayed

Daniel was consistent in his faith. Consistent enough that the presidents and princes knew he would continue to pray even if they could pass a law against it. If you were tried for praying, would there be enough evidence against you to convict you?

DANIEL'S CONFESSION
Vs 22

Of course Daniel was thrown into the den of lions. Someone pointed out that it was not just a lion's den. A lion's den might not have lions in it. This den was full of lions brother.

Daniel spent a whole night in the den and when the king came the next morning to see if Daniel had survived, he made the following.

A. My God
Darius had called Him Daniel's God. Daniel confessed it is truth: "God is indeed my God."
- He worshipped no other
- He owned God and God owned Him

There is a difference between
- **Knowing about God**
- **Knowing God**

Far too many know about Jesus. They have heard his story and may even believe it is true, but Jesus is not theirs and they are not His. Is the Lord your God? Are you sure?

B. God sent His angel to shut the lions' mouths
When God is your God
- **He will go with you everywhere**
- **He will be a help to you in all dangers**
- **He will stay with you at all times**

God's angel protected Daniel.
- **All night long**
- **In a den of lions**
- **From hungry lions**

We know these were fierce lions because they killed the princes and presidents after Daniel was lifted out. God's power is not some power over mystical things and spiritual things alone. God's power is over the natural things as well. The same God that we trust to forgive our sins can also be trusted to:
- **Deliver us from natural dangers**

- Calms the stormy seas of life
- Change the nature of His creatures for our protection

THIS DREAM TROUBLES ME

Daniel 7:1-28

The first six chapters of Daniel are historical in nature and concentrate on the subject of personal character. The last six chapters are prophetical in nature and deal with the veracity of the Scriptures.

The authorship of Daniel has been challenged by skeptics of the Bible because so many of its prophecies have been fulfilled with such accuracy that they say Daniel could not have written them before they happened. Daniel did write them under the influence of the Holy Ghost and their accuracy only proves to us, first, the inerrancy of Scripture and second, that we can trust those prophecies that have not yet been fulfilled will happen just as they are described.

Daniel chapter 7 deals with Daniel's dream of 4 beasts.
- **One like a lion with eagle's wings**
- **One like a bear with three ribs in the mouth**
- **One like a leopard with 4 wings and 4 heads**
- **One like no beast upon the earth**

Daniel had this dream in the first year of King Belshazzar.[11] So we know we have retraced our steps a few years. This is:

- **Before the Medes and Persians**
- **Before Kings Cyrus and Darius**
- **Before the Den of Lions**
- **Before Belshazzar saw the handwriting on the wall**

I want to take the chapter in three sections:

- **The Description of the Beasts**
- **The description of the King**
- **The meaning of it all**

THE DESCRIPTION OF THE BEASTS
Vs 4-8

Each one is amazing and unnatural but at least Daniel has some way to describe the first three:

A. A lion with eagle's wings
Vs 4

---

[11] Vs 1

- The wings were plucked off
- The lion stood like a man
- A man's heart was given to it

B. A bear raised on one side
Vs 5

- It had 3 ribs in its mouth
- It had command to devour

C. A leopard with 4 wings
Vs 6

- It had 4 heads
- It had a powerful dominion

D. Like nothing Daniel could describe
Vs 7-8

- Dreadful terrible
- Strong
- Iron teeth
- Ten Horns

- Another horn soon appeared

- It plucked off 3 horns

- The horn had eyes like a man
- The horn spoke great things (means domineering in character)

Daniel was still thinking through all of this when something else happened; *"thrones were cast down,..."*

Note
A DESCRIPTION OF THE ANCIENT OF DAYS
Vs 9-14

Notice first
A. His appearance
Vs 9-10

This sounds similar to Revelation 1:13-15
And in the midst of the seven candlesticks one like unto the Son of man, clothed with a garment down to the foot, and girt about the paps with a golden girdle.
His head and his hairs were white like wool, as white as snow; and his eyes were as a flame of fire;
And his feet like unto fine brass, as if they burned in a furnace; and his voice as the sound of many waters. (KJV)

B. His office
Vs 10

- He was over multitudes
- He served in the position of a judge
- He judged out of a book

Revelation 20:11-12

And I saw a great white throne, and him that sat on it, from whose face the earth and the heaven fled away; and there was found no place for them.
And I saw the dead, small and great, stand before God; and the books were opened: and another book was opened, which is the book of life: and the dead were judged out of those things which were written in the books, according to their works. (KJV)

C. The execution of His office
Vs 11-12

- The beast was slain
- His body destroyed

The other beasts were dethroned, but left alive for a time

D. The establishment of His Son
Vs 13-14

Note

THE MEANING OF THIS ALL
Vs 15-28

A. The four beasts are four kings in the earth
Vs 17

This is a repeat and expansion of Nebuchadnezzar's dream of the image. Each beast corresponds with one section of Nebuchadnezzar's image:
1. The lion is the golden head – Nebuchadnezzar and Babylon
- The lion is the king of beasts
- The eagle is the king of birds

Nebuchadnezzar's rule was a powerful one.

Wings plucked off is reminiscent of Nebuchadnezzar's humiliation (when he lost his mind and lived like an animal for seven years). Daniel 4:28-33

Made to stand reminds us of the restoration of his mind and his return to power. Daniel 4:36

Given the heart of man is reminiscent of his humility and his giving praise to the Lord – he probably got saved.

Daniel 4:37

B. The bear is the Medo-Persian Empire

Being raised on one side speaks of the fact that there was one half of this alliance (the Persians) that was more powerful than the other. Persia was the stronger, more aggressive part of this alliance.

The three ribs probably speaks of a three–nation alliance, between Babylon, Lydia and Egypt, headed by Egypt that attempted to defeat the Medo-Persians but lost.

C. The leopard is Greece – Under Alexander the Great
- **The four wings** typifies the speed with which he conquered the world.
- **The four heads** represents Alexander's four generals.
- **When Alexander the Great died**, his kingdom was divided up into 4 parts, each ruled by one of the four generals.

As you can see then, this is the image of Nebuchadnezzar in greater detail.

The bulk of the rest of the book of Daniel will be greater and great detail concerning,

D. The 4th beast
Vs 23-26

The fourth kingdom is the Roman Empire. It is different than the others in a number of ways:

1. Rome devoured the whole known world of its day
The other kingdoms controlled a majority of the world, but Rome completely subdued those nations under it.

2. Rome still controls the world
- **We use a Roman calendar**
- **We use a Roman time system**
- **We use a Roman base for our language**

Even today the Roman Catholic Church is still the only religious system in the world with diplomatic privileges. It is as if it were its own country. And the greatest majority of Christendom is dominated to some degree by Roman Catholic theology.

As a Baptist preacher my greatest challenge is to teach out of you the influence of the Roman Catholic Church in your thinking.
- **Universal Invisible Church**
- **Good Friday**
- **Fancy Religious ceremonies**
all trace back to Catholicism.

Unlike the previous Empires,

3. Rome was hated by its captives

Remember, Daniel served in the leadership of two of these Empires. Rome was

- **Very cruel**
- **Very corrupt**

Rome was never really defeated; she just ceased to be an influence. Her citizens became

- **So lazy**
- **So idol**
- **So self-serving**
- **So pleasure oriented**

that they just stopped mattering any more and eventually disbanded into little countries around Europe.

The ten horns would correspond to the ten toes in Nebuchadnezzar's image. It represents the coalition of ten kingdoms together to carry on the Roman Empire. Some have said that the *"European Common Market"* could be that ten king coalition. Others point to the **Euro Dollar** as a sign of this *League of Nations.*

I don't personally think it is wise to put too much emphasis on any of that. We know in God's time, there will be a ten-nation coalition

that revives the Roman Empire and we know that, **Out of that will arise one horn** – He will be the Anti-Christ.
Vs 25

- He will gain world power
- He will blaspheme God
- He will change "times and laws" (set up his own rule of law)
- He will "wear out" or persecute the saints
- He will do this for
    - A time   1 year
    - Times and   2 years
    - ½ time   ½ year

                            3 ½ years

But after 7 years he will be judged and destroyed by God.

I like the frankness of verse 26.
- There is an assurance in the verse
- There is a calmness in the verse

God is not concerned. God is not troubled. God has a plan and His infinite plan involves Anti-Christ. And it ends with his absolute and final destruction.

Conclusion
Vs 28

Daniel said all of this troubled and changed him. That's what studies about what God will do in the Tribulation should do to us. They should change us.

- **We should be troubled for the condition of the lost world**
- **We should be burdened for the direction the governments of this world are taking it**
- **We should proclaim to this world how they can be saved**

EPIPHANIES

Daniel 8:1-27

This chapter so accurately describes the fall of the Medo-Persian Empire to Alexander the Great that Biblical critics claim it could not possibly have been written by Daniel, but must have been written after Alexander died and was then inserted into Daniel's book.

This is the Third year of Belshazzar the king and Daniel has another vision. He saw first,

A RAM

Vs 3-4

The ram had two horns; one higher than the other but the highest horn came up last.

Daniel 8:20

The ram which thou sawest having two horns are the kings of Media and Persia. (KJV)

There is no question about the interpretation. This ram represents the kings of the Medo-Persia. The Medes would be the first horn. They conquered Babylon and started the Empire but the Persians soon arose with greater power.

The second horn, Persia, grew tallest.
Daniel 8:4
I saw the ram pushing westward, and northward, and southward; so that no beasts might stand before him, neither was there any that could deliver out of his hand; but he did according to his will, and became great. (KJV)

The ram pushes:
- **Westward**
- **Northward**
- **Southward**

but not
- **Eastward**

The Persians were as far east geographically as they could go without entering into the Oriental countries. The Orientals are a kind of boundary few in history have wanted to cross. So the Medo-Persian Empire pushed in every other direction to extend their kingdom. And they were successful. They did as they wanted – nothing withstood them.

Until,

THE HE-GOAT FROM THE WEST
Vs 5-8

A. His origination
"...from the West..."

Daniel 8:21 tells us exactly who this goat is.
And the rough goat is the king of Grecia: and the great horn that is between his eyes is the first king. (KJV)

This is of course Alexander the Great.

B. His successful operation
"...touched not the ground..."

When I was in High School, I had a 1969 Mustang Mach I. It had been my grandparents. Grandpa and Grandma Tiwater had a mustang they took to Arizona. When they came home they said it wasn't fast enough so they got the Mach I. When they died, I paid for the attorney to get their stuff out of probate and for that Mom and Dad gave me Grandpa's 30-06 Rifle and the Mach I.

Trouble was, I wasn't the greatest driver in the world. For the most part it was a waste for me to have the car.

- **I once got stopped for driving too slow on the highway.**
- **Another time I got pulled over in it because the patrolman thought I was too young to have a license.**

I did let some other guys in school race my car and it was by far the fastest car in Waitsburg High School at that time.

I only drove it fast one time. I was coming home from work late, late at night and on a particular strait stretch between Walla Walla and Waitsburg, I stepped on the gas a bit. When I got over 100 mph I got scared. It felt like I was flying. There were no bumps in the road. In fact the road was almost completely quiet.

I think that is what it means when it says the he goat "touched not the ground." It refers to how quickly he conquered and moved.

I did a little checking. They say that at the age of 32, Alexander the Great sat and wept "because there were no more kingdoms to conquer."

C. His conflict with the Medes and Persians
Vs 6-7

This is believed to be the battle between Xerxes and Alexander at Thermoplyae. (thuhr-MOP-uh-lee')[12] Xerxes had the greater force, an estimated 300,000 soldiers to Alexander's 110,000, but because Thermoplyae was a narrow pass, only a few could get through at a time.[13]

- **The Persian strength was in their numbers**
- **Alexander's strength was in the skill of his men**

His soldiers slaughtered the Persian army as they advanced through the pass. At the same time Xerxes had a fleet of 300 ships coming in behind Alexander. The entire fleet was destroyed by a storm. Alexander had conquered the world.

D. His destruction
Daniel 8:8

Therefore the he goat waxed very great: and when he was strong, the great horn was broken; and for it came up four notable ones toward the four winds of heaven. (KJV)

---

[12] http://en.wikipedia.org/wiki/Battle_of_Thermopylae, accessed 7-21-06
[13] J Vernon McGee, *Thru The Bible*, Vol 3, pg 578

While still very young and in his prime Alexander
- **Went on a night long drunk**
- **Caught a fever**
- **Died**

Belshazzar was destroyed in a drunken brawl. So was Alexander the Great.

Could be the same will happen to the United States.
- **Major decisions are made at cocktail parties**
- **President Reagan celebrated the end of his Presidency by drinking a beer on national television**
- **26,000 Americans are killed each year in drunk driving accidents**

E. The division of his empire
Vs 8

Once Alexander was dead his empire was divided between his four generals.
- **One took Europe**
- **Another took Asia Minor**
- **Another took Asia**
- **Another took Egypt**

Daniel's vision of
THE LITTLE HORN
Vs 9-14

We have this vision interpreted for us in
Daniel 8:23-25
And in the latter time of their kingdom, when the transgressors are come to the full, a king of fierce countenance, and understanding dark sentences, shall stand up.
And his power shall be mighty, but not by his own power: and he shall destroy wonderfully, and shall prosper, and practise, and shall destroy the mighty and the holy people.
And through his policy also he shall cause craft to prosper in his hand; and he shall magnify himself in his heart, and by peace shall destroy many: he shall also stand up against the Prince of princes; but he shall be broken without hand. (KJV)

A. The fierce king
Was Antiochus IV. He liked to call himself Antiochus Epiphanies which means "god manifest." He,
- **Attacked Jerusalem**
- **Attempted to exterminate the Jews**

When he captured the temple in Jerusalem, he set up the image of his god, Jupiter, inside and sacrificed a pig (an unclean animal) on the Jewish altar.

B. His likeness to the Anti-Christ
Daniel 8:24-25

And his power shall be mighty, but not by his own power: and he shall destroy wonderfully, and shall prosper, and practise, and shall destroy the mighty and the holy people.

And through his policy also he shall cause craft to prosper in his hand; and he shall magnify himself in his heart, and by peace shall destroy many: he shall also stand up against the Prince of princes; but he shall be broken without hand. (KJV)

There are those who believe Anti-Christ has manifested himself in human form many times over the history of humanity. They say that

- **Nimrod**
- **King Saul**
- **Antiochus IV**
- **Judas Iscariot**
- **Hitler**

were all pre-incarnations of the Anti-Christ. I don't really buy that. It is giving the devil nearly the same power as the Lord in not only possessing a man, but virtually becoming man. However Antiochus Epiphanies is without a doubt a foreshadow of what Anti-Christ will be like.

1. "His power shall be mighty, but not by his own power"
Vs 24

Antiochus did things that were almost unbelievable. His slaughter of the Jews rivaled Hitler. As I said, many believe both men were the devil incarnate. I am sure both were demon possessed. Antichrist will also conduct a great slaughter of the Jews through the power he has received from Satan.

2. "He shall cause craft to prosper in his hand"
Vs 25

Anti-Christ will control buying and selling. One of the most prominent things in the destruction of Babylon in Revelation 18 is that the people will weep because *"no man buyeth their merchandise any more."* Vs 11

3. "He shall magnify himself in his heart"
Vs 25

Revelation 13:3-6
And I saw one of his heads as it were wounded to death; and his deadly wound was healed: and all the world wondered after the beast.
And they worshipped the dragon which gave power unto the beast: and they worshipped the beast, saying, Who is like unto the beast? who is able to make war with him?

And there was given unto him a mouth speaking great things and blasphemies; and power was given unto him to continue forty and two months.
And he opened his mouth in blasphemy against God, to blaspheme his name, and his tabernacle, and them that dwell in heaven. (KJV)

4. "By peace he shall destroy many"
Vs 25

Anti-Christ will use a false world peace to gain world power. Then once gaining that power will use it to destroy the Jews and those that love the Lord.

5. "He shall stand up against the Prince of Princes."
Vs 25

"Anti-Christ" means "against Christ." This man will seek to destroy Christ.

6. "but he shall be broken without hand"

The Lord will not even raise a finger against Anti-Christ but will destroy him with the word of His mouth.

Signs of the times point the soon fulfillment of all of this. Praise the Lord that the rapture of the Christians happens first.

Are you ready if the Lord should come?

BY BOOKS

Daniel 9:1-2

Let me see if I can give you a time reference here.

Chapter 7:1 Daniel has a dream

It is the first year of the reign of Nebuchadnezzar's grandson, Belshazzar. Daniel says this dream "troubled" him and his countenance changed, but he kept it in his heart. (Vs 28)

Chapter 8:1 Daniel sees a vision

It is in the third year of the reign of Belshazzar. Daniel says this vision made him faint and sick. He was astonished [devastated] at the vision. (Vs 27)

Chapter 9:21 Daniel receives a visit from the angel Gabriel.

This is the first year of the reign of Darius, the one who defeated Belshazzar. But before he receives the visit, the Bible says Daniel "*understood by books*" the plan of God concerning the release of Israel from Babylonian captivity.

- **His dream had troubled him**
- **His vision had astonished him**

And the two of them had driven Daniel to study the "*books*."

These "books" are a reference to the written Word of God, which was then not completed, but certain ones of them had been finished (the Torah – first five books of the Bible and the Psalms for example). We are aware of at least one of the prophets whose writings were published by then because Daniel specifically mentions the Prophet Jeremiah in verse 2.

Scholars claim that by this time those portions of the Word of God which had been written, while not widely published, were in the hands of some private citizens.[14] Apparently Daniel was in possession of one of those private collections. What is even more apparent was that Daniel was in the habit of studying them.

THERE IS VALUE IN BOOKS

Of course I mean especially the Bible. This is only one instance in the Scriptures where the importance of reading is expressed. Admittedly a person has to think about it to see it but,

---

[14] E-Sword 7.7.7, *Albert Barnes' Notes on the Bible*, Albert Barnes (1798-1870)
It is sufficient to reply to it, that there is every probability that the Jews in Babylon would be in possession of the sacred books of their nation, and that, though the canon of the Scriptures was not yet completed, there would exist private collections of those writings.

A. The Gospel of Luke was given us after much research and reading.

Luke 1:1-3

Forasmuch as many have taken in hand to set forth in order a declaration of those things which are most surely believed among us,

Even as they delivered them unto us, which from the beginning were eyewitnesses, and ministers of the word;

It seemed good to me also, having had perfect understanding of all things from the very first, to write unto thee in order, most excellent Theophilus, (KJV)

Luke claims that the material he used to write his copy of the Gospel of Jesus Christ was

- **Those writings already published concerning Jesus' life**
- **Those eyewitness accounts he was personally familiar with**

He said that through them he had *"perfect understanding"* concerning the life story of Jesus Christ. That would have been through study.

B. Paul expressed a habit of reading too

2 Timothy 4:13

The cloke that I left at Troas with Carpus, when thou comest, bring with thee, and the books, but especially the parchments. (KJV)

Paul is sitting in a prison cell, awaiting his execution. What would be the most valuable things to him?

- **His coat – before winter (2 Timothy 4:21)**

- His books – he obviously didn't learn everything by revelation
- His parchments – most likely his copy of the written Word of God

C. Paul also urged others to be avid readers
1 Timothy 4:12-14
Let no man despise thy youth; but be thou an example of the believers, in word, in conversation, in charity, in spirit, in faith, in purity.
Till I come, give attendance to reading, to exhortation, to doctrine.
Neglect not the gift that is in thee, which was given thee by prophecy, with the laying on of the hands of the presbytery. (KJV)

- Daniel had dreams that troubled him
- Daniel had visions that astonished him

HOW DID DANIEL DEAL WITH THESE TROUBLING DREAMS AND ASTONISHING VISIONS?
By books….
- Not by television shows
- Not by gameboys
- Not by following
    - football
    - basketball
    - baseball

but *by books*

Proverbs 21:17

He that loveth pleasure shall be a poor man: he that loveth wine and oil shall not be rich. (KJV)

The Scriptures say that when a person loves pleasure, they become poor. Financially that is true because the financial resources are spent up in seeking the pleasure. Entertainment costs.

- **Is it $20.00 dollars to go to the movies yet?**
- **A night at Safeco could easily cost $150.00 per person**
- **How much does a person spend a day on the Ski Slopes?**
  - **Big screen TVs**
  - **The newest version of PlayStation**
  - **Travel expenses**
  - **Eating out**

You love that stuff very much and you'll be broke for sure!

Years ago I had a church member who was being harassed at work because he tithed. This fellow was calling him foolish to give so much money to the church. Brother Ward just challenged him, "Keep track of how much you spend on beer and cigarettes for a month. I'll bet it's much more than I tithe to church." And it was. Pleasure costs and those who love it and live for it are broke. But more than that, Americans have become a poor people.

- **Intellectually**

- **Emotionally**
- **Spiritually**

as well.

- **Our love for pleasure**
- **Our drive to indulge ourselves**
- **Our appetite for quick entertainment**

has left us a people with little use for books.

There is something different with books than any other form of entertainment.

A. Books require thought

A person can watch television with his mind completely turned off. Not so with books. Even a novel; a fictional book, requires thought. You have to conjure in your mind the:

- **Sights**
- **Sounds**
- **Smells**

described in books.

- **Your mind must decide what the character of the book looks like**
- **Your mind must give him or her a voice**

If the book is more technical, it requires even more thought.

Books, in order to read them require thought.

B. Books force introspection

You go inside yourself with a book.

- **If you are reading a story about an event in the 1800's you practically place yourself there.**
- **If you are reading a portion of Scripture that is convicting, you nearly have to point your finger at yourself.**

Reading is not a spectator event. It's just you and the book. You are more likely to benefit from reading. Even when reading out loud to a group, you can't read well for the benefit of the group. You must first read for your own benefit, and then those listening will receive benefit.

C. Books still the body

When you read you can't do anything else but read. Reading requires that you still the body and only read.

- **You can't drive and read**
- **You can't cook and read**
- **You can't talk on the phone and read**
- **You can't watch TV and read**
- **You can't mow the lawn and read**

You can only read and read. That has some health benefits right there, as well and emotional and spiritual ones.

THE BEST BOOK TO READ IS THE WORD OF GOD

Daniel didn't deal with his dreams and visions by reading

- **A romance novel**
- **A dime store western**

He was reading the book of books.

- **Sixty six books**
- **Written by more than 40 penmen**
- **Over the course of more than 1600 years**
- **With remarkable unity continuity**

The best thing we can read is the Word of God.

These books,

A. Answer our questions about the future

Daniel was reading the books and he discovered as He read the books that Jeremiah's book told specifically how long Israel would be in Babylon.

Daniel 9:2

In the first year of his reign I Daniel understood by books the number of the years, whereof the word of the LORD came to Jeremiah the prophet, that he would accomplish seventy years in the desolations of Jerusalem. (KJV)

We know exactly where he read that;

Jeremiah 25:12

And it shall come to pass, when seventy years are accomplished, that I will punish the king of Babylon, and that nation, saith the LORD, for their iniquity, and the land of the Chaldeans, and will make it perpetual desolations. (KJV)

Jeremiah 29:10

For thus saith the LORD, That after seventy years be accomplished at Babylon I will visit you, and perform my good word toward you, in causing you to return to this place. (KJV)

Daniel read that the captivity was supposed to last 70 years and those seventy years were just about over.

We are in captivity too.

- **Some of us are captives to sin**
- **Those of us who are saved are captives on this planet**

These books tell us:

- **How to be set free**
- **When we will be set free**

- **They tell us of hell and the future of those who are lost in sin**
- **They tell us of heaven and how to be free of sin so we can go there**

They answer our questions about the future.

These books,

B. Convict your conscience about sin

Danial 9:3-6

And I set my face unto the Lord God, to seek by prayer and supplications, with fasting, and sackcloth, and ashes:

And I prayed unto the LORD my God, and made my confession, and said, O Lord, the great and dreadful God, keeping the covenant and mercy to them that love him, and to them that keep his commandments;

We have sinned, and have committed iniquity, and have done wickedly, and have rebelled, even by departing from thy precepts and from thy judgments:

Neither have we hearkened unto thy servants the prophets, which spake in thy name to our kings, our princes, and our fathers, and to all the people of the land. (KJV)

And a person might say, "Why would I want to read something that got me under conviction?" Because it is only through conviction and then confession of sin that we can get things right with God. Having things right with God is always a wonderful thing.

How much better it is to be like Moses, begging God,

Exodus 33:18

....I beseech thee, shew me thy glory. (KJV)

Than to be like Adam and Eve when,

Genesis 3:8

... they heard the voice of the LORD God walking in the garden in the cool of the day: and Adam and his wife hid themselves from the presence of the LORD God amongst the trees of the garden. (KJV)

The Bible promises us,
I John 1:9
If we confess our sins, he is faithful and just to forgive us our sins, and to cleanse us from all unrighteousness. (KJV)

We can't confess that sin unless we know what it is and we get under conviction over it.

Daniel would not have known about the sin that had compelled God to send Nebuchadnezzar against Jerusalem if he had not learned it *"by books."*

These books,
C. Instruct us in skill and understanding
Daniel 9:20-22
And whiles I was speaking, and praying, and confessing my sin and the sin of my people Israel, and presenting my supplication before the LORD my God for the holy mountain of my God;
Yea, whiles I was speaking in prayer, even the man Gabriel, whom I had seen in the vision at the beginning, being caused to fly swiftly, touched me about the time of the evening oblation.

And he informed me, and talked with me, and said, O Daniel, I am now come forth to give thee skill and understanding. (KJV)

I am reminded that the Bible says,
2 Peter 1:3
According as his divine power hath given unto us all things that pertain unto life and godliness, through the knowledge of him that hath called us to glory and virtue: (KJV)

The instruction and skills we need for every area of life are all found in the Bible.
- How to find friends
- How to get a good job
- How to get raises and promotions
- How to find a good spouse
- How to be a good spouse
- How to raise kids to love and respect their parents
- How to be happy at all times
- How to live in peace with your neighbor
- How to be a good leader
- How to be a good follower
- How to be a good citizen
- How to be a good soldier
- How to be a good Christian

And even more. It's all found in the Bible. But it doesn't come to us by osmosis.

Daniel had likely been reading and studying the Word of God for the better part of 70 years when finally the Bible says he *"understood by books."*

Proverbs 25:2
It is the glory of God to conceal a thing: but the honour of kings is to search out a matter. (KJV)

God's design is that we spend a lifetime searching out the wonderful things found within the pages of these books.

Daniel 9:2
In the first year of his reign I Daniel understood by books ... (KJV)

A PRAYER OF REVIVAL

Daniel 9:1-19

As soon as Daniel understood what God was about to do, he was immediately burdened to seek the Lord through prayer. The prayer culminates in these inspiring words.

Daniel 9:19

O Lord, hear; O Lord, forgive; O Lord, hearken and do; defer not, for thine own sake, O my God: for thy city and thy people are called by thy name. (KJV)

Please notice with me three things concerning Daniel's prayer:

HIS CONVICTIONS IN THIS PRAYER WERE BIBLE BASED

Vs 2

They came after he "*understood by books.*" God's Spirit does not lead us outside of the Word of God.

John 16:13

Howbeit when he, the Spirit of truth, is come, he will guide you into all truth: for he shall not speak of himself; but whatsoever he shall hear, that shall he speak: and he will shew you things to come. (KJV)

A. A person, who does not know this book, does not know the leadership of God.

It seems to me that people are so flippant today concerning God that they will claim almost anything is the leadership of the Lord. People will do things that are downright contrary to the Bible and claim God supports it. Honestly sometimes it is tough to know.

1. During the civil war it is reported that someone asked President Lincoln if he thought God was on the side of the North. President Lincoln is reputed to have said, "My concern is not whether God is on our side, but if we are on God's side." Both the North and the South had strong arguments for the justice of their cause.

When you begin to study the history of the Civil War a little, you realize that the South had by far the more godly men in leadership
- **Robert Lee**
- **Stonewall Jackson**

Were both men of extreme spiritual passion. To this day there are Bible students who argue that the position of the South was the better position.[15]

---

[15] Recently an independent Baptist preacher (obviously from the South) recommended I read a book entitled *The South Was Right.*

2. Paul and Barnabas disagreed so strongly that they separated from each other in the work of the ministry. One thing I can promise you; God never leads you outside of the Word of God.

3. Years ago I was sitting among a group of preachers from Springfield, MO.
Springfield might be the most difficult town in America to be an independent Baptist preacher. Seems like half the students from Baptist Bible College felt the call of God to start a church – in Springfield.

These preachers were talking about a pastor who had fallen in sin and had to resign the church he pastured in Maine. He went down to Springfield to plant a new church there and went to Baptist Bible College to announce to the students that he was in town and invite them to come help him plant the church. The Executive Vice President of BBC opposed his announcing to the student body his new church. This pastor said, "You can't stop me from planting the church. I am led of God to do it." His response was, "And you can't stop me from banning your church to the student body, I am led of God to do it."

You see, to claim the leadership of the spirit in either case is a very tenuous position at best.

B. Do you have Bible to back what you claim to be the leading of the Spirit of God?

Or is it just what you want to do? I don't know how many people have sat in my office blaming God for not blessing a decision they made. They will boast to me that they knew it was God's will for their lives but I could give a dozens reasons why the decision they made was not according to Scripture.

Daniel was under conviction. And the conviction was brought on by study of God's Word.

DANIEL'S RESPONSE TO THIS CONVICTION WAS CONFESSION AND REPENTANCE
Vs 4-15

A. This portion begins with confession
Daniel 9:4
And I prayed unto the LORD my God, and made my confession,…. (KJV)

When you read the prayer in its entirety you see he both confesses for himself and for Israel as a whole. There is a place for both.

Years ago I heard Dr Jack Hyles tell a story that went something like this: John R Rice and Jack Hyles were preaching together in a meeting somewhere in the United States. Dr. Hyles went to Bro Rice's room to pick him up to go to the church. Brother Rice asked Brother Hyles to hang on a minute and Brother Hyles watched John Rice take a large sheet of paper, tear it into little bits and flush it down the toilet. When Brother Hyles asked him what he was doing, Bro Rice said, he had been confessing sins by writing them on a sheet of paper and asking God's forgiveness for them one at a time. Now that he had finished confessing those sins, he did not want anyone to get hold of them, hence tearing them up and flushing them down the toilet. Brother Hyles taunted Dr Rice a little about how large a list he had and at that moment Dr Rice said to him, "I wasn't confessing my sins, I was confessing yours." Maybe he could claim some Biblical authority for that practice in this passage.

I am grateful for 1 John 1:9
If we confess our sins, he is faithful and just to forgive us our sins and to cleanse us from all unrighteousness.
It's more than just a nice sentiment; it would be a wise thing to spend more time confessing our sins.

178

Notice also that this is more than just a simple apology to God.

B. There is a heart of repentance

Daniel says in Daniel 9:13

As it is written in the law of Moses, all this evil is come upon us: yet made we not our prayer before the LORD our God, that we might turn from our iniquities, and understand thy truth. (KJV)

Daniel saw that is was necessary not only to apologize but also to turn from iniquities.

We have to stop blaming God for our sins; "I asked God to help me quit my sin and He didn't." The fact of the matter is that if you are saved God has already given you everything you need to quit your sin. It is now up to you to decide to do it. If you are saved,

- **You have the indwelling Holy Spirit**
- **You have the infallible Word of God**
- **You have the local church of God**
- **You have your preacher**

And if you will let them have the place in your life they are supposed to have, you can defeat your sin.

Judges 18:7 KJV

Then the five men departed, and came to Laish, and saw the people that were therein, how they dwelt careless, after the manner of the Zidonians, quiet and secure; and there was no magistrate in the land, that might put them to shame in any thing; and they were far from the Zidonians, and had no business with any man.

There were four reasons why the Danites decided the city of Laish would be an easy target to defeat:

- **They dwelt carelessly** – they weren't looking for an enemy
- **They had no magistrate** – they were as sheep without a shepherd
- **They had no accountability** – there was no discipline to help them do right
- **They had no support** – they did not have good friends to lift them up in times of temptation

- **If we won't be vigilant, looking for Satan to trap us**
- **If we won't follow our pastor's leadership**
- **If we won't be disciplined about living for God**
- **If we won't choose good friends**

We have no right to blame God when we fail in sin.

HIS REQUEST WAS FOUNDED IN GOD'S RIGHTEOUSNESS and not his own
Vs 16

I don't know what it is like in the rest of the world. I do know that one of the best sales tactics in America is to say something to the effect of *"Go ahead, you deserve it."*

- **You deserve a new car**
- **You deserve a new spouse**
- **You deserve a break today**
- **You deserve to be happy**
- **You deserve a face lift (I saw it advertised on a billboard on Canyon Road not too long ago)**

The reason why pointing out that we deserve it works to get us to buy things is because, well, we believe we do deserve it.

Many times that is exactly the way we approach the Lord. "God

- **I deserve to be happy**
- **I deserve a better job**
- **I deserve your answers to my prayers**
- **I deserve to be just as well off as my neighbor"**

Daniel approached prayer completely differently than that. He asked God to answer,

- **Not because Daniel deserved it**
- **Not because Israel deserved it**

but because God is righteous. That changes everything.

- It changes what you ask for, no more consuming it upon your own lusts
- It changes your reaction to the answers to prayer, no more getting upset when God doesn't answer how we want him to
- It changes why we ask for the things we ask for

We are not asking for it for ourselves. We are not asking for it for what we can get out of it. We are asking for it.
- According to God's righteousness
- For His glory

SEVENTY WEEKS

Daniel 9:20-27

Prophetically speaking, there is no passage in the Bible more important than the one before us.

Daniel had been stolen from his family and from his home as a young man, probably in his early teens. He had been taken to Babylon and trained there for service to Nebuchadnezzar the king. But Daniel's

- **Strength of character**
- **Purity of life and especially**
- **Devotion to his God**

had so set him apart from others that he became a leader in the government, not only of:

- **Babylon, but of the**
- **Medes and the**
- **Persians as well**

Now Daniel is an old man. Seventy years have passed since he was stolen away from his home. As he studied the books, the Word of God, Daniel realized that God had revealed through the Prophet

Jeremiah that the captivity and exile of the Jews, that Daniel was a part of, was only supposed to last seventy years.

So Daniel set himself to prayer, seeking that the Lord would do as His Word had promised. It was during this time of prayer that God sent Gabriel to tell Daniel what His plan for Israel was.

KEYS TO UNDERSTANDING THIS PROPHECY
The first one being that
A. This prophecy concerns Daniel's people, Israel
Daniel 9:24

Seventy weeks are determined upon thy people ... (KJV)

"Notice that these need not be consecutive weeks. The time did not begin until Israel was back in their land with their own worship national life.
When [in 70 AD] they would be scattered...the time would not be counted....The time is seventy weeks of national Jewish history."[16]

It is key that we keep in mind that God's plan for the ages revolves around Israel. There is a place for the Gentiles in God's plan, but we ~~must remember to keep them~~ separate. Even in this day when God is

[16] John R Rice, *The Second Coming of Christ in Daniel*, pg 28

calling out a people from every nation, kindred tongue and tribe the church does not replace Israel in God's plan.

The seventy weeks determined in the passage have to do specifically with Israel.
Daniel 9:24
... to finish the transgression, and to make an end of sins, and to make reconciliation for iniquity, and to bring in everlasting righteousness, and to seal up the vision and prophecy, and to anoint the most Holy. (KJV)

B. Each week equals seven years
While our culture only thinks of a week in terms of days, it was a very natural part of Old Testament Jewish culture to view a week as any one of several series of sevens.

For instance, Exodus 23:10-12
And six years thou shalt sow thy land, and shalt gather in the fruits thereof:
But the seventh year thou shalt let it rest and lie still; that the poor of thy people may eat: and what they leave the beasts of the field shall eat. In like manner thou shalt deal with thy vineyard, and with thy oliveyard.
Six days thou shalt do thy work, and on the seventh day thou shalt rest: that thine ox and thine ass may rest, and the son of thy handmaid, and the stranger, may be refreshed. (KJV)

Be careful not to force your mentality into the Word of God. Israel would have no difficulty viewing a week as seven years. For the sake of Bible interpretation neither should we.

DANIEL'S SEVENTY WEEKS
Daniel 9:25-27

Gabriel divided the seventy weeks into three distinct groups:
A. Seven weeks
Daniel 9:25
... that from the going forth of the commandment to restore and to build Jerusalem unto the Messiah the Prince shall be seven weeks, ..., even in troublous times. (KJV)

The Bible says that the first seven weeks will begin with the commandment to restore/rebuild Jerusalem and the Bible scholars believe that the passage means that the reconstruction process will last seven weeks – or 49 years. And the Bible says that the process will happen during "troublous times."

Read Nehemiah and Ezra and you will learn that the rebuilding process was during troublous times. The days were so dangerous that Nehemiah 4:17 says,

They which builded on the wall, and they that bare burdens, with those that laded, every one with one of his hands wrought in the work, and with the other hand held a weapon. (KJV)

The second division is a period of
B. Sixty-Two Weeks
Daniel 9:25-26
Know therefore and understand, that from the going forth of the commandment to restore and to build Jerusalem unto the Messiah the Prince shall be seven weeks, and threescore and two weeks: the street shall be built again, and the wall, even in troublous times.
And after threescore and two weeks shall Messiah be cut off, but not for himself: and the people of the prince that shall come shall destroy the city and the sanctuary; and the end thereof shall be with a flood, and unto the end of the war desolations are determined. (KJV)

Not much information is given to us about this sixty-two weeks except that the Bible says that,
1. The Messiah will come and be suddenly *"cut off."*
Notice it says that it won't be for Himself. Jesus Christ came into this world and lived a short 33 years. His ministry lasted only 3 ½ years. He was captured in the middle of the night, rushed through one mock trial after the other and then executed on a cross in haste so He could be dead and buried before the Jewish Passover.

The Word of God is very clear. He did not die for any crime He had done. Isaiah 53:5

But he was wounded for our transgressions, he was bruised for our iniquities: the chastisement of our peace was upon him; and with his stripes we are healed. (KJV)

The Bible says of this sixty-two week period that,

2. The city and sanctuary will be destroyed

An event that took place in 70 AD with the Roman General Titus conquered Jerusalem and leveled the city. Before the atrocities were done most of the Jews had fled the area. Those who remained were driven to a plateau known as Masada where they committed suicide rather than being taken by the Romans.

We can put with some accuracy,

3. Dates to these 69 weeks.

With regarding the dates, there are a couple of questions that come into play:

a. Which commandment to rebuild Jerusalem do we go by?

There were three.

Cyrus

Ezra 1:1-2

Now in the first year of Cyrus king of Persia, that the word of the LORD by the mouth of Jeremiah might be fulfilled, the LORD stirred up the spirit of Cyrus

king of Persia, that he made a proclamation throughout all his kingdom, and put it also in writing, saying,
Thus saith Cyrus king of Persia, The LORD God of heaven hath given me all the kingdoms of the earth; and he hath charged me to build him an house at Jerusalem, which is in Judah. (KJV)

Darius
Ezra 6:1
Then Darius the king made a decree, and search was made in the house of the rolls, where the treasures were laid up in Babylon. (KJV)

Ezra 6:8
Moreover I make a decree what ye shall do to the elders of these Jews for the building of this house of God: that of the king's goods, even of the tribute beyond the river, forthwith expenses be given unto these men, that they be not hindered. (KJV)

Cyrus made the decree that the temple be rebuilt. Enemies succeeded in getting the work stopped until Darius searched and ordered the work resume.

Artexerxes
Nehemiah 2:1-8

And it came to pass in the month Nisan, in the twentieth year of Artaxerxes the king, that wine was before him: and I took up the wine, and gave it unto the king. Now I had not been beforetime sad in his presence.

Wherefore the king said unto me, Why is thy countenance sad, seeing thou art not sick? this is nothing else but sorrow of heart. Then I was very sore afraid,

And said unto the king, Let the king live for ever: why should not my countenance be sad, when the city, the place of my fathers' sepulchres, lieth waste, and the gates thereof are consumed with fire?

Then the king said unto me, For what dost thou make request? So I prayed to the God of heaven.

And I said unto the king, If it please the king, and if thy servant have found favour in thy sight, that thou wouldest send me unto Judah, unto the city of my fathers' sepulchres, that I may build it.

And the king said unto me, (the queen also sitting by him,) For how long shall thy journey be? and when wilt thou return? So it pleased the king to send me; and I set him a time.

Moreover I said unto the king, If it please the king, let letters be given me to the governors beyond the river, that they may convey me over till I come into Judah;

And a letter unto Asaph the keeper of the king's forest, that he may give me timber to make beams for the gates of the palace which appertained to the house, and for the wall of the city, and for the house that I shall enter into. And the king granted me, according to the good hand of my God upon me. (KJV)

We are going to settle on Artexerxes' command as the one meant in Daniel, because it is the one that was not to rebuild the city and not just the temple.

The second question has to do with,

b. How do we date his commandment?

Rather than trying to get into the details of the difficulties let's just settle it that we have a pretty accurate ten-year window. I am going to use one of the more popular of the several dates proffered:

- **454 BC which would have the first seven weeks conclude by**
- **405 BC and would have the sixty two weeks conclude around**
- **29 AD**

Calendars are not accurate for that period of time but we know that Jesus began His ministry right around 29AD and was crucified right around 31 AD. Daniel's prophecy is pretty accurate!

C. One final week to cover
Daniel 9:27

And he shall confirm the covenant with many for one week: and in the midst of the week he shall cause the sacrifice and the oblation to cease, and for the overspreading of abominations he shall make it desolate, even until the consummation, and that determined shall be poured upon the desolate. (KJV)

This final week begins when a prince shall come and confirm a covenant with Israel for one week – seven years. Notice there is a difference:

- **There is Messiah the Prince (capital "P")**
- **There is the prince (lower case "p")**

This is the Antichrist, and this final week is also referred to as the Great Tribulation. He will establish a seven year peace treaty in Israel.

- **Israel will be allowed to rebuild their Temple (they haven't got one today**
- **Israel will restore their Old Testament worship (they don't do that even today)**

But then, in the middle of the week, he will break his own covenant, forcing Israel to cease worshipping the Lord and to begin worshipping himself.

By the end of the week, Israel will finally turn to Christ and Jesus will return.

Danial 9:24

... to bring in everlasting righteousness, and to seal up the vision and prophecy, and to anoint the most Holy. (KJV)

You will notice that we have a huge gap between the end of the 69th week and the beginning of the 70th week. It is because during this period Israel has no national identity. They haven't had since approximately 70 AD. They are a great people, but they did not exist in their Promised Land until after WWII. Even today, their national identity is not what it was in the Old Testament.

- **A Muslim mosque sits on the mount where the Temple is supposed to be**
- **Jerusalem is partially occupied by Islamic Canaanites and**
- **Israel as a nation is more of a secular presence rather than a spiritual one**

Ezekiel 37:8 prophesies of this when Israel will come together as a body but have:

- **No breath**
- **No life**
- **No spirit**

They won't live as a spiritual nation again until the Tribulation period.

Today God is doing something completely different. He has not replaced Israel, but He has put them aside for we sometimes call the Church Age. It is an indeterminable period of time when the Lord is calling out of every nation tongue and tribe, the church – a bride for Jesus Christ. And it will end with the rapture of those saints to glory.

Once the saints are gone, the Lord will take up where He left off in dealing with the Jews.

WHAT ARE WE SUPPOSED TO DO TODAY?

There are three key things Christians are supposed to occupy themselves with during this age:

A. Walk worthy of the Lord

Ephesians 4:1

I THEREFORE, the prisoner of the Lord, beseech you that ye walk worthy of the vocation wherewith ye are called. (KJV)

Colossians 1:9-10

For this cause we also, since the day we heard it, do not cease to pray for you, and to desire that ye might be filled with the knowledge of his will in all wisdom and spiritual understanding;
That ye might walk worthy of the Lord unto all pleasing, being fruitful in every good work, and increasing in the knowledge of God; (KJV)

1Thessalonians 2:11-12

As ye know how we exhorted and comforted and charged every one of you, as a father doth his children,
That ye would walk worthy of God, who hath called you unto his kingdom and glory. (KJV)

Every Christian should devote himself to learning the Word of God and disciplining themselves to live life in a way that is worthy and pleasing to the Lord.

B. Work at accomplishing the Great Commission
Matthew 28:18-20

And Jesus came and spake unto them, saying, All power is given unto me in heaven and in earth.

Go ye therefore, and teach all nations, baptizing them in the name of the Father, and of the Son, and of the Holy Ghost:

Teaching them to observe all things whatsoever I have commanded you: and, lo, I am with you alway, even unto the end of the world. Amen. (KJV)

Our primary motivation in life ought to be to please the Lord and our primary duty in life ought to be to try to win souls to Christ and get them baptized into church where they can be taught to please the Lord.

C. Watch for Jesus' soon return
Titus 2:11-13

For the grace of God that bringeth salvation hath appeared to all men,

Teaching us that, denying ungodliness and worldly lusts, we should live soberly, righteously, and godly, in this present world;

Looking for that blessed hope, and the glorious appearing of the great God and our Saviour Jesus Christ; (KJV)

- **Our primary motivation in life ought to be to please the Lord**

- Our primary duty in life ought to be to try to win souls to Christ and get them baptized into church where they can be taught to please the Lord and then
- Our primary attitude ought to be "looking up" with our eyes fixed toward the skies
  - waiting
  - longing
  - hoping that

perhaps today will be the day Jesus comes again.

DANIEL'S 70 WEEKS

Daniel 9:1-27

Many consider this one of the greatest chapters in the whole Bible. In it Daniel is given the prophecy of 70 weeks.

Note first
Daniel's Preparation
Vs 2

Daniel is close to 90 years old at this time. He was taken captive approximately 606 BC. Darius became king around 537 BC. So it has been 69 years in captivity. In that 69th year Daniel read and understood the words of Jeremiah the prophet that the Jews would be in captivity 70 years (Jeremiah 29:10)

Then Daniel began to pray.
Vs 3

Note that the determining factor that got Daniel to prayer was the study of the Word of God. This should not be taken negatively but

positively. One cannot know God's will nor be in God's will if he or she does not study God's Word.
- **This is the foundation of the Christian life**
- **This is the guide that God has given**

If you do not study the Bible consistently you are out of God's will. I can't make a Christian study the Bible but God can't use a Christian that doesn't.

Daniel studied God's word and found in Jeremiah what God's plan was.

DANIEL'S PRAYER
Vs 3-19

Daniel's prayer is composed of three parts which will help us in composing our prayers. I do believe in spontaneous prayer. But I also see planned prayer in the Scripture; prayer with a purpose, not just idle repetitions and flowery phrases.

This prayer is made up of
Confession
Vs 4-6

Declarations
Vs 7-14
Petitions
Vs 15-19

A. Daniel was specific in confession of Israel's sin and his own
It's not good enough to just says "God, I have sinned." We need to be willing to confess to God each sin.

B. Daniel spent time praising God, glorifying God with declarations.
It is good to show God that we believe He is right in all His judgments.

C. Daniel brought His petitions and requests.
In verse 20 while Daniel was still praying, the angel Gabriel came to Daniel with

DANIEL'S PROHECY OF 70 WEEKS
Vs 20-27

Remember that Daniel was praying because he knew that the 70 years of Jewish captivity in Babylon were about over when Gabriel came with the message that more trouble was coming. Actually the day of the 70 year captivity is finished in the beginning of the 70 week judgment.

One of the hard things to grasp is how long is a week. We automatically think of 7 days. However the Jews had a:
- **7 day week**
- **7 year week**

Leviticus 25:3-4

The 70 years of Babylonian captivity were a chastisement from God for not obeying the Sabbath years.[17] For 70 of those "weeks" Israel had ignored the Sabbath year. God made them leave the Promised Land to give the land those missing 70 Sabbath year rests.

Now right in the middle of Daniel's thinking about all of this, Gabriel says "70 weeks are determined upon the people". When you take into consideration all this is supposed to happen in these 70 weeks, it has to be longer that 490 days. We are talking about 70 weeks of years.
- **1 week=7 years**

---

[17] 2 Chronicles 36:20-21

- 70 weeks=490 years

The 70 weeks are then divided into 3 periods
- 7 weeks
- 62 weeks
- 1 week

Verse 24 tells us the purpose of the 70 weeks. In other words, Israel would suffer national chastisement for 490 years in order that God could:
- Make an end of Israel's sin
- Make reconciliation for her sin
- Bring in everlasting righteousness

Let's now break these 70 weeks apart to see what is in them.

A. Seven weeks or forty nine years

To restore and to rebuild Jerusalem
Vs 25

Ezra, and Nehemiah were written to describe this rebuilding project; a project riddled with problems delays and persecutions. Malachi wrote during this time and so the Old Testament was completed during these 49 years.

B. Sixty two weeks or four hundred thirty four years

The Bible is silent during these years. This is the period between the Old Testament and the New Testament. During those years Alexander the Great took dominion of the world from the Medes and the Persians. Antiochus Epiphanes slaughtered many Jews and defiled their Temple. Rome took the world from the Greeks and Herod the Great was appointed King in Israel by Rome.

Israel went through some terrible wars during those 62 weeks. But it was nearing its end when Matthew wrote of the birth of our Lord Jesus Christ.

Notice Daniel 9:26
"And after three score and two weeks shall Messiah be cut off,…"
The 62 weeks ended with the death, burial and resurrection of Jesus Christ the Messiah.

C. The seventieth week does not begin immediately

Ephesians 3:1-12
1 Peter 1:10-12

Daniel knew nothing of the "church age." You and I live in a period of:
- **Unknown duration**

202

- **Unforeseen by the Old Testament prophets.**

It began with the death of Jesus Christ and it will end with the Rapture. This Rapture is important. If it does not happen before the "70th" week of Daniel, then we who are alive will suffer during that time.

I believe strongly that the Bible teaches a "pre-tribulational" rapture. In other words, that all the Christians will be taken out of this world before the Tribulation which is Daniel's 70th week.

Scriptures used here are
- **1 Thessalonians 4:13-18**
- **2 Thessalonians 1:7 and 2:7-8**
- **Revelation 3:10 and 4:1**

Note that after Revelation 4:1 the word church is not used again in Revelation. I believe that is because the church is no longer on the earth.

D. The seventieth week is seven years
We call it the Tribulation period.

That seven year period is broken into two parts; the first 3 ½ years Antichrist will be a false prince of peace. He will use peace to gain world power. In the middle of the week, 3 ½ years later, he will turn on those who gave him power. I believe it is because he will have the power he feels he needs to force the world to worship him as God.

In my opinion the event that will turn him will be the battle of Gog and Magog.
Ezekiel 38-39

Russia (Gog and Magog) will attack Israel and God will destroy them. Once Russia is no longer a threat to Antichrist he will begin his terrible persecutions until the Lord Jesus Christ returns. When Christ returns He will destroy the armies of Antichrist and cast him into the lake of Fire. Then Christ will establish His own kingdom of everlasting righteousness, thus fulfilling the purpose for the 70 weeks
(Daniel 9:24)

THE VISION, THE VISITOR AND THE VERIFICATION

Daniel 10:1-21

We are quickly approaching the end of Daniel's prophecy. This chapter introduces and sets up the prophecy of chapters 11-12.

THE VISION

Vs 1-9

A. A Specific Time

Vs 1

This is one of those places in the Bible when we are given a specific date and time. This was in the 3rd year of Cyrus, King of Persia. Ezra 1:1 tells us that the Babylonian captivity ended in the first year of Cyrus' reign.

Daniel was over 90 years old by this time. We know from history that very little happened in the first two years of Israel's release.

Daniel must have been heartsick. In verse 2 we find him mourning and fasting for three weeks – 21 days. It was in this period of mourning and fasting that he saw a vision of the Glorified Lord.

He calls Him,
B. A certain man
Vs 5

It is interesting how many times the Lord referred to Himself or to the Heavenly Father as a certain man or a certain king.

- **Matthew 18:23**
- **Matthew 21:28**
- **Matthew 22:2**
- **Mark 12:1**
- **Luke 13:6**
- **Luke 14:16**

and more. We couldn't use this as conclusive proof that Daniel's vision is of Christ and I sure would not say that every time a "certain man" is used in the Gospels it refers to Jesus Christ

Let's compare Daniel's vision here with John's vision in Revelation 1:12-15

- **Both mention clothing**
- **Both have a gold girdle**
- **Both have "eyes of fire"**

- Both have "feet of polished brass"
- Both have "voluminous voices"

Although the descriptions are not word for word, it is obvious they are both describing the same Person; the Glorified Jesus Christ.

Also notice in both cases,

3. The reaction to the vision

Revelation 1:17 has John falling at His feet as dead.

From Daniel 10 vs 7-9

a. Those with Daniel left him alone

The closer we get to the Lord the fewer friends we will have in this world. Very few are willing to become truly faithful Christians. If you make that choice, you will find that as you draw close to the Lord, your friends, even Christian ones, will seem to forsake you. There will be plenty of times when you are left alone with God. But you will also find that He is a great person to be left alone with. Experiencing being alone with Christ is actually one of the great blessings of a close walk with the Lord; once you get used to having fewer close earthly friends.

The vision caused Daniel

b. To go unconscious

Vs 8-9

It is a very healthy thing to come to the place of realizing how unworthy we are of Christ. The fear of the Lord is the beginning of knowledge. But God didn't suffer either John or Daniel to stay down. In both cases these men were quickly stood to their feet.

God does not intend for us to be so afraid of Him that we can't move. He wants us to get up and work and worship. There are people who won't do anything for the Lord because they are afraid of making mistakes.

There is an old saying, "The man who never makes mistakes; never does anything." I am convinced that God would rather we make mistakes in an effort to serve Him than for us not to serve at all.

Notice with me
THE VISITOR
Vs 10-13

This is an un-named angel, but my guess is that it is Gabriel. The angel left heaven, it says, 21 days before he finally arrived at Daniel's side.

A. There is a reason for delayed answers to prayer

The angel had been sent to Daniel 21 days before this but was held up by the unseen forces of darkness. God was using this for His purpose

We must realize that Satan does not want your prayers answered. Therefore if he can keep you from praying or keep your prayers from being answered, he will have won in his mind. Truth be told, he can't keep a prayer from being answered, so really the only way he can be victorious is if he can keep you from praying.

There is an invisible war going on between the forces of Heaven and the forces of darkness. We are not given many details in the Bible about this war, only enough to know it is going on. The human prince of Persia could be no match or even a hindrance to an angel or archangel. This prince of Persia is its fallen Angel-Leader.

Remember that Satan possesses the kingdoms of this world.
Matthew 4:8-9
Again, the devil taketh him up into an exceeding high mountain, and sheweth him all the kingdoms of the world, and the glory of them;
And saith unto him, All these things will I give thee, if thou wilt fall down and worship me. (KJV)

This "prince" is Satan's assigned demon to protect the devil's interests in that kingdom. Other passages tell us about the war between the angels; fallen and holy

Revelation 12:7-9

And there was war in heaven: Michael and his angels fought against the dragon; and the dragon fought and his angels,
And prevailed not; neither was their place found any more in heaven.
And the great dragon was cast out, that old serpent, called the Devil, and Satan, which deceiveth the whole world: he was cast out into the earth, and his angels were cast out with him. (KJV)

Jude 1:9

Yet Michael the archangel, when contending with the devil he disputed about the body of Moses, durst not bring against him a railing accusation, but said, The Lord rebuke thee. (KJV)

- **Some people want to believe in the Lord but not in Satan.**
- **Some want to believe in angels but not in demons**
- **Some want to believe in Heaven but not in Hell**

This one sided type of belief is contrary to the Bible. Accept it all, or not at all.

There is a spiritual battle going on and we are smack dab in the middle of it.

Ephesians 6:11-12
Put on the whole armour of God, that ye may be able to stand against the wiles of the devil.
For we wrestle not against flesh and blood, but against principalities, against powers, against the rulers of the darkness of this world, against spiritual wickedness in high places. (KJV)

That's why Paul told Timothy,
2 Timothy 2:3-4
Thou therefore endure hardness, as a good soldier of Jesus Christ.
No man that warreth entangleth himself with the affairs of this life; that he may please him who hath chosen him to be a soldier. (KJV)

Do you believe it or not? We are not supposed to be "mamsy pamsy" about this stuff. We are supposed to acknowledge the spiritual battle going on and prepare ourselves to "war a good warfare."[18]

I am as bad as anybody about this I guess because I love my church and want to protect you like a good pastor. But we are "babied" way too much these days. When the battle comes our way, we aren't generally tough enough to take it.

---

[18] 1 Timothy 1:18

Daniel's visitor told him he had to hurry and get back in the fight.
Vs 20

THE VERIFICATION
Vs 14-21

This is where the prophecy of the chapter begins, and it is really a summary of what is explained in chapters 11-12.

A. There are three features to the vision
Vs 14

1. It concerns the people Israel
2. It will be accomplished in the "latter days"
which is undoubtedly Daniel's 70th week.
3. "Yet the vision is for many days"
Which tells us that a long period of time is involved. It will be many days before this prophecy is fulfilled.

B. Daniel was visibly sorrowed over the vision
Vs 15-17

So the angel gave him comfort.

Vs 18-19
"O man, greatly beloved, fear not:…"

Wouldn't you like to be known in heaven as "greatly beloved?" We can be! Oh that we would:
- **Love God**
- **Serve God**

Not so much that we would be the most productive, but that we would be the most loving of Christ.

C. The importance of the Bible
Vs 21
Even when the angel speaks, he speaks the truths of the Word of God. The Bible is truth and cannot be contradicted.
- **Not by a preacher who claims to have a vision**
- **Not by an angel**
- **Not by you and me**

May we be students of the truth.

THE WAR BETWEEN NORTH AND SOUTH

Daniel 11:1-20

Chapters 11 and 12 of Daniel continue to describe the vision Daniel had in chapter 10. This vision was important enough that the angel that revealed these things to Daniel was delayed 21 days by Satan.[19] These two chapters are going to tell us some of the details of the 70 weeks prophesied by Daniel in chapter 9.

- **Daniel 11:1-36 is history**
- **Daniel 11:37-12:13 is prophecy**

Remember when Daniel recorded these things, it was all prophecy. None of this happened in Daniel's lifetime. We find recorded in Daniel 11:1-36 what happened between the writing of the Old Testament and the New Testament. The Old Testament ends with the beginning of Daniel's 70 weeks; with Israel leaving Babylonian captivity and going back to rebuild Jerusalem. Historically we know much of what happened from then until Christ was born. But not biblically the Bible was completed (Old Testament) and so, was silent for over 400 years.

------

[19] Daniel 10:12-13

Daniel's prophecy about the 400 years however, has been so accurate that those who deny the truthfulness of the Bible say Daniel could not possible have written this. They think like this:

- **Miracles are impossible.**
- **There are no such things as miracles.**
- **For Daniel to have been able to record such an accurate prophecy about the 400 years between the Old and New Testaments would be a miracle.**
- **Since miracles are impossible Daniel must not have written the Daniel chapter 11.**

FOUR MORE KINGS

Daniel 11:2 says four more kings will reign in Persia after Darius.

- **Ahashuerus Cambyses**
- **Artaxerxes Psuedo-Smerdis**
- **Darius Hystaspis**
- **Xerxes (He was "the notable one." In 480 BC he invaded Greece but was defeated by Alexander the Great.)**

Alexander the Great is foretold in verses 3-4. Alexander had conquered the world by 335 BC. However in 323 BC he died of Pneumonia after a night of drunkenness. His own posterity did not inherit his kingdom. Instead it was divided into four areas controlled by four of his generals.

- Cassander to Europe
- Lysimchus took what is modern Turkey
- Seleucus took Syria
- Ptolemy took Egypt

THE WAR BETWEEN NORTH AND SOUTH

Vs 5-20

The story narrows down here to just two of the four generals, the kings:

- **Of the south**
- **Of the north**

You should ask the question, "North and South of what?" The answer is *"The Promised Land"* especially Jerusalem. God views Jerusalem as the center of the world and in the Bible you will find that everything is north, south, east west, up or down of Jerusalem.

- **The kingdom that was directly south of Jerusalem was Egypt, under the Ptolemy's.**
- **The king of the north would be Syria under Seleucus and his family.**

And Israel is right in the middle.

History records this incredible story:

Vs 6

In order to have peace between Syria and Egypt one of the Ptolemy's named *Philadelphus* gave his daughter *Bernice* to marry one of the Seleucies named *Antiochus*. The problem was Antiochus was already married. So he divorced his first wife and married Bernice. They had a son. After a time Bernice's father, the Ptolemy, King of Egypt, died. So Antiochus divorced Bernice and re-married his first wife who then:

- **Poisoned him**
- **Executed Bernice and her son**
- **Set her own son on the throne**

By this time Bernice's brother was the reigning Ptolemy in Egypt and a war broke out between Syria and Egypt. Just as we read Daniel 11:7-8, the Ptolemy of Egypt won that war. History says he came home with:

- **4000 talents of gold**
- **40,000 talents of silver**
- **2500 idols**

Verse 8

In those days if one country was fighting another country, you didn't fly your troops over and parachute them into the battle arena. You marched into battle and you took everything you needed to supply your troops off the land you were marching through. Consequently

Israel became the stomping ground for or else the battleground for countless battles between Egypt and Syria and the land of Israel was nearly decimated.

I understand that the fortress in the valley of Megiddo, near Nazareth was rebuilt and destroyed 20 times during these battles. Historians say that Israel went from a lush paradise to almost desert wasteland primarily because of these battles between Egypt and Syria.
Verses 15-20

THE RAISER OF TAXES

Eventually there was a treaty made between Syria and Egypt.

Most of us are at least a little familiar with this story. It is during the days of *Cleopatra* and *Mark Antony*. Once relative peace was established Syria set out to conquer the western kingdom including Greece and Rome.

Verse 19-20
Syria loses the war and Rome is established as the great world empire of the day. The passage mentions taxes. J Vernon McGee said that only one nation has ever rivaled Rome in raising taxes, the

United States of America. The Roman Empire was virtually built on the taxes they got from those nations they conquered.

Verse 20 says Rome is not completely in power. It is still only the western region of the 4 Grecian parts. We still have one more significant story to be told from the kingdom of the north of Israel.

ANTIOCHUS EPIPHANES
Vs 21-36
I referred to him in a message out of Daniel 8 as "the little horn" that came out of the four horns. Antiochus Epiphanes is an historical character but he foretells what the Antichrist will be like.

Verse 21
He is a vile person
He came to power under a program of peace but they were all lies and flatteries. They say that during his reign, 100,000 Jews were slain. He defiled the Jewish temple by sacrificing a pig on their altar and setting up an idol to Jupiter there.

Those were terrible days in Israel

Rome was gaining power and Antiochus was taking out his anxieties upon the Jews. The ships of Chittim, vs 30 (a reference to the Roman Navy) had prevented Antiochus from conquering Egypt.

But in the midst of all the terror in Israel
verse 32.

This could easily be a reference to a Jewish family by the name of the Maccabees. This family raised a revolt that eventually led to the fall of Antiochus Epiphanes and the rededication of the Temple. Around Christmas the Jews celebrate Hanukkah. It is their celebration of the Maccabean defeat of Antiochus and the cleansing of their Temple. Soon after that Rome conquered the world and Israel came under their hand.

As I have said earlier. The prophesies in the Word of God are not there simply to satisfy man's curiosity about the future. God gave prophetical information to demonstrate that His Word is true and being true we should:
- **Believe it**
- **Obey it**
- **Preach it to others**

FINAL MESSAGE

Daniel 11:36-12:13

The Tribulation is the last week of Daniel's 70 week prophecy. It is a period of seven years of trouble such as this world has never seen. It will begin, praise God, right after all of us who have accepted Christ as Saviour are raptured into heaven. It will end with the physical return of Jesus Christ to the earth to establish His kingdom.

ITS LEADER

Daniel 11:36-45

We get the name Antichrist from 1 John 2:18.

Little children, it is the last time: and as ye have heard that antichrist shall come, even now are there many antichrists; whereby we know that it is the last time. (KJV)

It refers to a man who is empowered by Satan and who gains almost total world domination. I personally believe he will be a Jewish descendent because of Daniel 11:38. I also believe he will be a Pope because of Revelation 17-18, but we won't get into that.

By the way, it should not be startling to think of the Pope as Jewish. The Roman Catholics think (although fallaciously) that the first Pope was Peter, a Jew.

A. He will be totally self-willed
B. He will magnify himself and blaspheme God
C. God will allow him to prosper for a while
Vs 36

Notice that, even during this time, God is in control. He allows Antichrist to prosper.

D. He will not regard the God of his fathers
Vs 37

He will not worship as they did. He will probably carry out wickedness against all forms of organized religion.

E. He will not have the desire of women
Vs 37

Catholic celibacy - not interested in:
- **Love**
- **Marriage**
- **Sex**

This also could mean he is homosexual.

Jack Chick has written a series of articles – now more than 25 years old - in a comic book format that are based on interviews with an ex-Catholic priest named Alberto Rivera. In them Jack Chick and Alberto Rivera accuse the Roman Catholic system to be rife with both immoral sexual activity among the priests and nuns and homosexual activity. Certainly the homosexual pedophiliac problem in the Roman Catholic system has been exposed in the news since then.

F. His god will be the god of force
Vs 38
He will rule by force and power

G. He will be attacked by the kings of the north and the south
Vs 40
Russia and Egypt. I believe this will happen at the middle of the Tribulation. God will destroy especially Russia[20] and Antichrist will begin the Great Tribulation.

H. He will not be able to defeat (control) Edom or Moab
Vs 41

---

[20] Ezekiel 38-39

There is a hidden city in the rocks and caves of Edom called Petra. I believe that many Jews will flee to Petra from Antichrist and God will protect them there.

Revelation 12:14
And to the woman were given two wings of a great eagle, that she might fly into the wilderness, into her place, where she is nourished for a time, and times, and half a time, from the face of the serpent. (KJV)

I. He will conquer Egypt and go there
Vs 42-43

K. While in Egypt he will hear news that troubles him
Vs 44

I think he hears about the return of Jesus Christ in the heavens. Jesus' return is gradual and visible and He will return with the armies of heaven following Him. I think this will be a very dramatic event. I think the news stations will broadcast the strange things they see in the skies. Someone will recognize that this is fulfillment of prophecy concerning the Christ. The whole event will be gradual enough that Antichrist will have time to gather his armies and prepare for the battle of Armageddon.

L. He is destroyed in the battle by the King of Kings and no one can help him.
Vs 44-45

Revelation 19:11-21

And I saw heaven opened, and behold a white horse; and he that sat upon him was called Faithful and True, and in righteousness he doth judge and make war.

His eyes were as a flame of fire, and on his head were many crowns; and he had a name written, that no man knew, but he himself.

And he was clothed with a vesture dipped in blood: and his name is called The Word of God.

And the armies which were in heaven followed him upon white horses, clothed in fine linen, white and clean.

And out of his mouth goeth a sharp sword, that with it he should smite the nations: and he shall rule them with a rod of iron: and he treadeth the winepress of the fierceness and wrath of Almighty God.

And he hath on his vesture and on his thigh a name written, KING OF KINGS, AND LORD OF LORDS.

And I saw an angel standing in the sun; and he cried with a loud voice, saying to all the fowls that fly in the midst of heaven, Come and gather yourselves together unto the supper of the great God;

That ye may eat the flesh of kings, and the flesh of captains, and the flesh of mighty men, and the flesh of horses, and of them that sit on them, and the flesh of all men, both free and bond, both small and great.

And I saw the beast, and the kings of the earth, and their armies, gathered together to make war against him that sat on the horse, and against his army.

And the beast was taken, and with him the false prophet that wrought miracles before him, with which he deceived them that had received the mark of the beast, and them that worshipped his image. These both were cast alive into a lake of fire burning with brimstone.

And the remnant were slain with the sword of him that sat upon the horse, which sword proceeded out of his mouth: and all the fowls were filled with their flesh. (KJV)

Daniel 11 takes us all the way through to the end of the Tribulation. As we come to Daniel 12 we go back through the Tribulation with more detail.

M. Michael the Archangel is seen fighting against Satan
Vs 1
Revelation 12 describes this battle. Michael seems to be the guardian of the nation of Israel. I believe he will be the one who protects the Jews hidden at Petra.

N. The Two Resurrections
Vs 2
There are two resurrections described here. From other portions of Scripture, we know that this happen 1000 years apart. The just refers to the Old Testament believers and to those who died during the Tribulation. At the end of the Tribulation and the beginning of Christ's 1000 year reign on this earth these believers (saints) will be

resurrected to live on earth during that reign. They will then and there enjoy everlasting life.

The unjust will be resurrected at the end of the 1000 year reign of Christ. Daniel says *"to shame and everlasting contempt."* It is described in Revelation 20:11-15.

And I saw a great white throne, and him that sat on it, from whose face the earth and the heaven fled away; and there was found no place for them.

And I saw the dead, small and great, stand before God; and the books were opened: and another book was opened, which is the book of life: and the dead were judged out of those things which were written in the books, according to their works.

And the sea gave up the dead which were in it; and death and hell delivered up the dead which were in them: and they were judged every man according to their works.

And death and hell were cast into the lake of fire. This is the second death.

And whosoever was not found written in the book of life was cast into the lake of fire. (KJV)

ITS LENGTH
Vs 5-12

You will note that there are three time periods given to us
A. Time, times and half a time
Vs 6-7

- Time = one year
- Times = two years
- Half= ½ year

For a total of 3 ½ years. Most of what we think of when we think of the Tribulation happens in the final 3 ½ years of the 7 year period.

B. 1290 days
Vs 11

Using the Jewish year of 360 days, this equals 3 ½ years, plus 30 days. Although this is only speculation, I believe it is reasonable to assume that the 30 days extra is the time used by the Lord to divide what He calls the sheep from the goats.

Matthew 25:31-46
When the Son of man shall come in his glory, and all the holy angels with him, then shall he sit upon the throne of his glory:
And before him shall be gathered all nations: and he shall separate them one from another, as a shepherd divideth his sheep from the goats:
And he shall set the sheep on his right hand, but the goats on the left.
Then shall the King say unto them on his right hand, Come, ye blessed of my Father, inherit the kingdom prepared for you from the foundation of the world:
For I was an hungred, and ye gave me meat: I was thirsty, and ye gave me drink: I was a stranger, and ye took me in:

Naked, and ye clothed me: I was sick, and ye visited me: I was in prison, and ye came unto me.

Then shall the righteous answer him, saying, Lord, when saw we thee an hungred, and fed thee? or thirsty, and gave thee drink?

When saw we thee a stranger, and took thee in? or naked, and clothed thee?

Or when saw we thee sick, or in prison, and came unto thee?

And the King shall answer and say unto them, Verily I say unto you, Inasmuch as ye have done it unto one of the least of these my brethren, ye have done it unto me.

Then shall he say also unto them on the left hand, Depart from me, ye cursed, into everlasting fire, prepared for the devil and his angels:

For I was an hungred, and ye gave me no meat: I was thirsty, and ye gave me no drink:

I was a stranger, and ye took me not in: naked, and ye clothed me not: sick, and in prison, and ye visited me not.

Then shall they also answer him, saying, Lord, when saw we thee an hungred, or athirst, or a stranger, or naked, or sick, or in prison, and did not minister unto thee?

Then shall he answer them, saying, Verily I say unto you, Inasmuch as ye did it not to one of the least of these, ye did it not to me.

And these shall go away into everlasting punishment: but the righteous into life eternal. (KJV)

- The sheep are those who lived through the Tribulation and are believers
- The goats are the unbelievers not killed in the natural disasters that had happened during the Tribulation or in the Battle of Armageddon

229

Joel describes people lined up for miles awaiting their turn to be judged.

Joel 3:1-2

For, behold, in those days, and in that time, when I shall bring again the captivity of Judah and Jerusalem,
I will also gather all nations, and will bring them down into the valley of Jehoshaphat, and will plead with them there for my people and for my heritage Israel, whom they have scattered among the nations, and parted my land.
(KJV)

C. 1335 days
Vs 12

This is the same 1290 days with another 45 days added to it. Again we can only speculate but we speculate that this time is used by the Lord after the judgment of the sheep and the goats to establish His government. We know that we will rule and reign with Him. Believers will be made rulers over:

- **Cities**
- **Counties**
- **Regions and even**
- **Nations**

Luke 19:12-19

He said therefore, A certain nobleman went into a far country to receive for himself a kingdom, and to return.

And he called his ten servants, and delivered them ten pounds, and said unto them, Occupy till I come.

But his citizens hated him, and sent a message after him, saying, We will not have this man to reign over us.

And it came to pass, that when he was returned, having received the kingdom, then he commanded these servants to be called unto him, to whom he had given the money, that he might know how much every man had gained by trading.

Then came the first, saying, Lord, thy pound hath gained ten pounds.

And he said unto him, Well, thou good servant: because thou hast been faithful in a very little, have thou authority over ten cities.

And the second came, saying, Lord, thy pound hath gained five pounds.

And he said likewise to him, Be thou also over five cities. (KJV)

Revelation 2:26

And he that overcometh, and keepeth my works unto the end, to him will I give power over the nations: (KJV)

One commentary says that the 75 days from the end of the Tribulation to the beginning of the 1000 year reign is similar to the United States system where the President is elected in November but does not take office until January 20; approx. 70 days later. During this time the newly elected President is appointing those who will serve under him in various capacities.

THIS LEAD INTO THE TRIBULATION
Vs 4

There are two signs given to Daniel that precede the Tribulation.
A. An increase in speed
"many shall run to and fro..."

Isaac Newton who was a believer, said in 1680, "Men shall travel from country to country in an unprecedented manner. They may even invent machines that can reach speeds in excess of 50 miles per hour." Fifty years later the atheist Voltaire those words and wrote, "Newton actually writes that men may travel at the rate of 30 or 40 mph! Has he forgotten that if a man traveled at this rate he would be suffocated? His heart would stand still!"

Jets now commute us around at several hundred miles per hour. Rockets have taken men to the moon at speeds over 17,000 miles per hour.

B. An increase in knowledge
Education is the emphasis of our day almost and in fact defied. Man's technology has leaped in just a few years. Though few in number now, there are people still alive today:

- Who have seen technology take us from horse and buggy to space shuttles.
- Who have known a day when a trip to Grandma's house 25 miles away was as difficult a trip as a trip to Denver 1200 miles away would be now.

Though not here in Daniel, the Bible gives us at least five more signs that the Tribulation is near:

1. Increase in wars and rumors of wars
Matthew 24:6
And ye shall hear of wars and rumours of wars: see that ye be not troubled: for all these things must come to pass, but the end is not yet. (KJV)

2. Extreme Materialism
2 Timothy 3:1-2
This know also, that in the last days perilous times shall come.
For men shall be lovers of their own selves, covetous, boasters, proud, blasphemers, disobedient to parents, unthankful, unholy,(KJV)

3. Departure from the Christian faith
1 Timothy 4:1
Now the Spirit speaketh expressly, that in the latter times some shall depart from the faith, giving heed to seducing spirits, and doctrines of devils; (KJV)

4. Lawlessness

2 Timothy 3:3-4

Without natural affection, trucebreakers, false accusers, incontinent, fierce, despisers of those that are good,
Traitors, heady, highminded, lovers of pleasures more than lovers of God;
(KJV)

5. Increase in religious cults

Matthew 24:4-5

And Jesus answered and said unto them, Take heed that no man deceive you.
For many shall come in my name, saying, I am Christ; and shall deceive many.
(KJV)

I do not believe in passing out information. The point of Bible preaching, teaching and study is to cause us to do something. That is exactly how the book of Daniel ends; Daniel 12:13

But go thou thy way till the end be: for thou shalt rest, and stand in thy lot at the end of the days. (KJV)

go thy way till the end be:...

In other words, "Occupy until Jesus comes." There will be a day of rest and we will have our reward in the end. But today we are to occupy. We are to take what the Lord gives us in the Word of God and tell as many people as we can what it says.